WITH

ROD AND LINE

IN

COLORADO WATERS

Lewis Browne France

photo courtesy of the Colorado Historical Society

WITH

ROD AND LINE

IN

COLORADO WATERS

*Wha ever heard o' a gude angler being
a bad or indifferent man?*
— Noctes

BY

L. B. FRANCE

PRUETT PUBLISHING COMPANY
BOULDER, COLORADO

Copyright © 1884 by Chain, Hardy & Co.
Foreword © 1996 by John H. Monnett
First Pruett Publishing Company printing: 1996

ALL RIGHTS RESERVED. No part of this book may be reproduced without written permission from the publisher, except in the case of brief excerpts in critical reviews and articles. Address all inquiries to: Pruett Publishing Company, 2928 Pearl Street, Boulder, CO 80301.

Printed in the United States of America
10 9 8 7 6 5 4 3 2 1

Library of Congress Cataloging-in-Publication data

France, Lewis B., 1833–1907.
    With rod and line in Colorado waters / by L. B. France.
      p.   cm.
    Originally published: Denver : Chain, Hardy & Co., 1884.
    ISBN 0-87108-881-9 (pb)
    1. Fly fishing—Colorado. 2. Colorado—Description and travel. I. Title.
    SH475.F735 1996
    917.880431—dc20   96-7164
                                                                     CIP

Cover and book design by Jody Chapel,
Cover to Cover Design

Contents

Foreword	vii
Publisher's Note	xii
Many Years Ago	1
Over the Range	9
Fisherman's Luck	18
Agapae	28
Black Lake in 1878	36
Egotism and — Rods	50
Troublesome	57
Meteorological	64
Mules	72
Music and Meteorology	79
Philosophy	89
An Idle Morning at Grand Lake	97
Camping with Ladies and — the Baby	104
Boys and Burros	113
He's No Sardine	133
Under Difficulties	140
His Sermon	151

FOREWORD

Lewis Browne France was the first important outdoor writer in the Rocky Mountain West. Born to a comfortable family in Baltimore on August 8, 1833, he attended private schools, graduated from Georgetown University, and studied and practiced law in Chicago. In 1861 he married Rowena Hewitt of Elgin, Illinois.

Like so many newlyweds of the time, the Frances were lured to the western frontier believing they would find opportunity. They migrated to Gold Rush Denver in that same year 1861. Denver was still a crude settlement devoid of comforts as well as badly needed services. The couple moved into an unchinked log cabin near present-day Fifteenth Street, now the historic district of the city. Since legal services were in great demand on the mining frontier France had no trouble finding clients. He and his family prospered. When Colorado achieved statehood in 1876, France was appointed reporter to the state Supreme Court and later he served as a district judge.

But Lewis B. France is remembered not for his legal career but for his engaging tales of fly fishing in the wilderness of the Rocky Mountain West, especially Colorado. From the 1880s until his death in 1907, his articles and essays appeared in national sporting journals such as *The American Angler* and *Outdoor Life*. Though overshadowed in the more populous east by contemporaries like George Dawson, George "Nessmuk" Sears, and the renowned Theodore Gordon, Lewis B. France introduced many sportsmen of the Gilded Age to the streams and high lakes of the Rocky Mountains.

France wrote two books at the height of his career which did more to make the world aware of the angling life in the Rocky Mountain West than any publications before that time. *With Rod and Line in Colorado Waters* (1884), republished here after more than a century, is considered a regional classic. France's sequel, *Mountain Trails and Parks in Colorado* (1887) addresses other topics besides fishing. Excerpts from both books were utilized by various railroad companies in tourist books and brochures designed to attract sportsmen to the narrow gauge routes through the high country, the most successful of which was the Colorado Midland's *History of a Line: From Plains to Peaks, Fishing and Hunting in Colorado* by Horace A. Bird.

France's prose is often times wordy by modern standards of outdoor writing, but we must remember that he was a product of Civil War era romanticism. As such his metaphorical style was favorably received by the sentimentally attuned readers of the Victorian Age.

But France differed from other writers of the era in one major respect. Lengthy, enamored descriptions of mountain scenery and battling big fish in the contemporaneous style of the era's "me and Joe" stories was not the primary goal of this pioneer outdoor writer. France was more interested in people, the fate of man, and his angling prose helped open up the American West and the temper of its populace to a growing number of readers. Improved human endeavor and a deeper knowledge of man's relationship with the natural environment were the literary aims of Lewis B. France.

This is not surprising given France's time and place in the history of the American West. Living through the gold rush and the transformation of Denver from a primitive settlement to a western metropolis and state capitol, there is little doubt that France was perplexed by the paradox of industrial and social progress and a shrinking wilderness. In the span of a decade he witnessed the near extinction of greenback cutthroat trout along Colorado's Front Range. He saw them replaced with exotic imported species through unregulated stocking. Little wonder then his writing is suggestive of Thoreau's transcendentalism. More and more over the years France stressed man's responsibility to nature. As such, France's later essays flew in the face of frontier mentality which placed emphasis on how nature's bounty could serve man.

France's angling tales appeared regularly in the

pages of *Western World*, a Denver based booster magazine slanted toward tourists and potential migrants to Colorado. France wrote a column titled "Scraps" for this magazine under the curious pen name *Bourgeois*. In 1899 the best of his "Scraps" columns were published in a book of the same name.

But *Western World* was a typical booster publication. As such it painted an idyllic picture of life in the Rocky Mountain region. Often it stressed the abundance of fish and game resources awaiting the sportsman. In his later years, the overall tone of this booster press disturbed France. By 1900, his articles began to include opinionated assessments of current fish and game regulations and his perceived need for additional protection. So concerned was Lewis B. France with the relationship between man, sport, and nature, that the *Denver Times* dubbed him the Poet Chronicler of the Rockies.

He took his concerns even further. In the Dickensian tradition of the era France often invited influential friends to the spacious parlor of his Denver home where he would read aloud from his books. His readings were often supplemented with discussions over cigars about the ethics of fishing and proper behavior for true sportsmen. During this time environmental conservation became more and more important to the aging attorney and he used his influence in the courts and the state legislature to bring about revisions in fish and game laws, which became some of the most progressive codes in the West. Thus France's legacy is more than mere entertainment of appreciative readers.

Today Colorado takes pride in its outdoor sporting tradition—and its environmental consciousness—begun by Lewis Browne France. Its continued enrichment and efforts toward preservation is fitting tribute to the man who first told the world about angling in the Rocky Mountains.

John H. Monnett
Boulder, Colorado 1996

Publisher's Note

This classic collection of angling stories was first published over a century ago. As such, it reflects the political values and attitudes of the 19th century American West, including the hostile frontier sentiments toward Colorado's Native Ute population. To preserve the historical integrity of this work, we reprint it here as it originally appeared, unedited and in its entirety (save for minor stylistic changes). Though the instances are few, the book contains some language that today's audiences will find distasteful or offensive, especially with respect to the Ute people who, we recognize, inhabited and celebrated the majesty of the Rocky Mountain West long before France and those of his time.

*Poor drudge of the city! how happy he feels
With the burs on his legs and the grass at his heels;
No Dodger behind, his bandannas to share;
No Constable grumbling: "You must n't walk there!"*
—Holmes

Many Years Ago

ORTY years ago — a big slice off the long end of one's life! A broad river with its low-lying south shore heavily timbered and rich in early summer verdure; a long bridge with a multitude of low stone piers and trestlework at top; in midstream, two miles away, the black hull and tall masts of a man-o'-war, lying idly; between and beyond, the smooth bosom of the blue expanse dotted with fishing sloops under weather-beaten wings, moving lazily hither and yon; to the north, but invisible save a straggling outer edge of tumble-down houses — a possibility then — now, "they tell me," a magnificent city; a decayed wharf with no signs of life, and draped in tangled seaweed that came in with the last tide, the jagged and blackened piles stand brooding over the solemn stillness like melancholy sentinels sorrowing over a dead ambition. The ripple of the waves is a melody and the air is fragrant with a brackish sweetness.

It has been a bright day, and the afternoon shadows are beginning to lengthen. They suggest to some another day's work nearly finished, another week drawing to a close; Saturday night, home and rest. To others they suggest—well, let that pass. To a little fellow, barefoot, coatless and with a ragged straw hat, who crawls out from one of the center piers of the old bridge, these shadows of the closing May day are ominous, yet his forebodings are not unmixed with the rose-hued pleasure of a day well spent. He did think of that river below him, twenty-five feet deep, but that was an attraction. He did think of the very near future and—but no matter; his thoughts were bright enough as he hauled up after him a string of perch as long as his precious body, and as a fit climax to his magnificent catch, an eel at least two and a half feet long and thick as his captor's arm. What a struggle he had enjoyed with that eel before he got it to the top of the pier. His handline was a hopeless snarl; twice he had come within a hair's-breadth of going overboard, but the unfortunate eel had succumbed to juvenile activity and zeal. What ten-year-old could boast comparison, as with the day's trophies over his shoulder he plodded his way home? He felt himself an object of interest and envy to his fellows, and told with condescension, not arrogance, his experience with that eel.

Success will often take an old boy, let alone a young one, off his feet; it sometimes leads to indiscretion and results in worse than failure, and again is the cornerstone of a noble monument. That boy had fished with success off that pier more than once, but had kept his fishpole and had left the evidences of his disobedience at a friendly neighbor's. This day he marched straight home, fishpole and all. The sable ruler of the kitchen confirmed, upon sight, the lurking apprehension that would not down in spite of triumph.

"Ah, honey! Whar's you bin dis livelong day? Miss Mary's gwine to give it to you. We's been ahuntin' an' trapsin' all ober dis here town, an' yo' pa—he was jes gwine—."

But the "ambiguous givings out" of the sable goddess were cut short by the appearance of Miss Mary in person. She was a stately dame in those days, with a wealth of dark hair and with brown eyes that had in them, ah, such a world of love for that barefoot, white-haired urchin. And she had, too, a quiet way of talking that went right into the little fellow's ears and down about his heart and lingered there. No need to ask him where he had been; she only looked at him and the fish, a serious, yet a loving look withal, took his hand and led him in to the head of the family. Court was at once convened.

"What *shall* we do with this boy?"

He to whom this inquiry was addressed took

in the situation at a glance. The glance was a dark one, but it quickly showed the silver lining.

"Wash him, and give him some clean clothes."

"But," she remonstrated, "this will never do; he will be drowned some day. How often must I forbid you going near the river?"

"I dun'no, mother."

"What is that round your leg?"

"An eel skin."

"Why did you tie it there?"

"To keep off cramp."

"Keep off cramp! What does the boy mean?" There was a look of wonderment in the brown eyes, and of merriment in the grey. The colored member of the court volunteered an explanation, and wound up with the prophecy:

"Dat chile'll neber be drownded, Miss Mary; I tell you so long as he wear dat eel skin he'll nebber hab de cramp, an' he kin swim; you ha'ar me, Miss Mary. Why, bless yo' stars, honey, dat child done swim dat ribber las' Saturday, he did; I heerd 'em tellin' it."

"Heard who telling it?" broke in the president.

"Why, de chillum, ob cose. Dat Buckingham boy he bantered the chile an' took his close ober in de skiff, and Mar's Lou, he done follered, he did, an' dat ribber a mile wide."

The animated and confident manner of Jane did not lessen the anxious, even horrified, expression in the brown eyes, but the grey were a study as the owner drew the abashed urchin to him, with the inquiry:

"Is it true, my boy?"

"Yes, father."

"Go bring me your fishing tackle."

It was a sorry looking outfit—a fraction of a cane pole, about ten feet of a common line, and an indifferent hook looped on the end. The handline was of better material, but a wreck—a very Gordian knot. They were dubiously but promptly passed over for inspection.

"Throw these into the stove—and, Jane, you make kindling wood of this pole."

"Oh, father!" The boy's lips quivered, the eyes filled, but the owner of the grey eyes gently held back the appealing hand that would have rescued the precious treasures.

"Hold on, my boy; do not misunderstand; papa will trust you; you shall have the best tackle in town."

"Why do you deal with the boy in this way?" remonstrated his mother.

"Why? Because I myself was a boy once, and I don't want to forget it."

The grey eyes were the first to close—it is many a long year since—and the old boy's fill a little now, as he reverently thinks of that day.

But the boy drifted with the tide, over the Blue Ridge and the Alleghenies, and twenty odd years ago he anchored in the wilderness, where

Denver now stands, to surprise you folks from down East.

Do we have fishing in the Rocky Mountains? Aye, that we do, and right royal sport it is.

One day, nineteen years ago this summer, a neighbor came into my cabin and wanted to know of a young married woman there if she could not spare her Benedict for, say three days. He was fish hungry, this neighbor; was going off into the mountains, and wanted company. Of course she could; was glad to be rid of him. And so early next morning old Charlie was hitched to the buckboard. At five o'clock that same day there was a tent pitched in a little valley upon Bear Creek, thirty-five miles from home, with two pairs of blankets, a coffee pot, two tin cups and a frying pan; not a soul or a habitation within twenty miles of us; a beautiful mountain stream, clear as crystal, cold as ice, and teeming with trout. What would you have, money? Why, bless your soul, money was at a discount; there were acres of it a little way off, only for the digging.

In those days fishing tackle was scarce, and a plumbush pole and linen line were the best in the land. Flies were a novelty to me, but my friend had a dozen or so, some that he had saved over from more civilized times, and that had got out here by mistake. He divided with me, told me to fasten one upon the end of my line and "skitter it over the water." This was my first and only instruction in trout fishing. "Skittering" was as novel to me as the fish, but my Professor was a Cambridge man with glasses, and I did not want him to feel that my education had been entirely neglected. I took my pole and instruction in silence, and walked a quarter of a mile up the creek. Pure instinct? Yes, I walked up stream for the single purpose of fishing down; it came just as naturally as swimming in deep water. I found a place clear of bushes for a few rods, where the current swept directly into my shore and out again, forming an eddy. I thought it a "likely place." I gave that plum sapling a swing and landed the fly, in which I had no confidence whatever, just at the edge of the swirl. It had no sooner touched the water than I saw a salmon-colored mouth, felt a tug, and the following second my first trout was flying over my head. I deliberately put down that pole and walked out to investigate. There was no doubt about it; there he lay, kicking and gasping his life out on the green grass, his bright colors more beautiful by the contrast. He was near a foot long, and I put my hand upon him as gently as though he had been an immortal first born. It was not a dream. When he was dead I strung him upon a forked stick, went back to the eddy and caught three others, and wondered if all the trout in that stream were twins. I had already become gentler, too, even with the unwieldy plum sapling. I found their mouths were not made of cast iron nor copper lined. By the time

I had fished down to camp, and with my ten trout, I felt equal to the business of the morrow. My friend, of course, had better luck, having passed his novitiate, but he complimented me in saying that I "took to it naturally."

Camping out was no novelty, but fresh trout was a revelation, and that night we had no bad dreams under our canvas. The next evening found us preparing nearly, what a Yankee would call, two patent pails of trout to take home to our friends and neighbors.

And here I am moved to say that ours is a noble fellowship; it is a gentle craft we cultivate, one that should beget brotherly love and all things charitable; and if any of you have, as I hope you have, a little white-haired tot who seems inclined to follow you downstream upon summer days, do not say nay, but let your prayer be: "Lord, keep my memory green."

Over the Range

OF course it is never agreeable to go camping; it is not convenient to carry about with one bedsteads, chairs, bureaus, washstands, bath-tubs, and such like plunder deemed essential to comfort. And then again it is not comfortable to live out doors like a tramp. It is either too hot or too cold, too dry or too wet—that is for a certain large class of human beings. They wonder why one will forego the comforts of our civilized ways for those of the Ute. But perhaps we may get to the solution of the problem further on.

It was dusty when our party left Idaho for a fifty-mile drive to Hot Sulphur Springs. Of course it was dusty; the dust was in the road, in our eyes and mouths, throats and lungs, just for our discomfort, and the tollroad companies were never known to keep sprinklers. So we traveled in a cloud for half an hour, then it began to rain. Of course it did; the first rainstorm for three weeks; we got damp, then we forgot the dust, and were doggedly satisfied that if pleasure had not been one of our objects in going camping it would not have rained. We got to Empire; it rained till dark, and everybody said the rainy season had begun in earnest, that it was liable to keep on raining for three weeks to get even with the "dry spell," and we went to bed feeling very much encouraged. There is an exasperating sententiousness about the mountain weather prophet that prevails nowhere else on the globe, I verily believe; when he tells you what the weather is, or is going to be, you must believe him. You dare not even express a hope that he may be mistaken. But even this gentry, one soon begins to believe, is essential to comfort; the weather prophet is the means of agreeable disappointment. Our weather prophet was the most entertaining old liar that ever contributed to the misery of a tenderfoot or the mortification of a mossback. The sun never broke over the eastern hills more gloriously than on the eventful next morning; he seemed to come up in a spirit of exultation, as if aware that the prophet at Empire had been maligning him. But the prophet was not overcome; far from it; the appearance of the sun was a "weather breeder," and the cheerful old atmospheric vaticinator swore that before we could reach the summit of the range it would and must rain, and snow and hail and freeze and thaw and blow and the —. We bade him good morning sadly, and took the road with a determination to wrest comfort, if necessary, from the worst "spell of weather" the range could boast.

The rain of the day before was the first element to lend its influence to the day's enjoyment; it had sweetened the air, if Colorado mountain air is ever otherwise; it had laid the dust, and the road was a marvel of excellence—for a toll road; it had sharpened the fragrance of the pines, and the wild flowers, lacking in perfume, made amends by such a wealth of beauty that one became lost in the multitude of bright colors.

We were a happy party that rode up through the Devil's Gate to encounter punishment. Leaving the magnificent mass of granite cliffs reaching a thousand feet high, and wondering if he who should follow next would experience the same degree of veneration for the mighty pile, we began the ascent of Berthoud Pass. We did not climb; there is no climbing to be done, except one escapes over a precipice, and has an ambition to get back. Strolling leisurely along, the white-capped range would, from time to time, reveal itself through the green of the pines, while to the left of us plunged down from the snowy heights the beautiful mountain stream, here not degraded and a satire on its name. Its banks are fringed with rich-colored mosses and decked with flowers, and the beautiful firs, waved by the gentle breeze, seemed to be bowing an accompaniment to the music of the crystal waters at their feet. As we go on, the sharp ridge of Red Mountain comes into view, guarded on the east by a monster hill, which none of our ingenious explorers, so generous in giving names, have condescended to dignify with a title. Its broad base washed by the rushing torrent, its sides clothed in a mantle of living green away up to the sharp line which marks the limit of the timber growth, and yet on and up the eye glances over the granite, with its azure background, until the vast pile is diademed with a fleecy cloud. It is a noble mountain, and involuntarily I took off my hat to it, wondering if the civil engineers, explorers, and the like, had really the monopoly of the love and veneration for the beautiful. Red Mountain! a carmine-colored excrescence dignified with a name, and this overtopping evidence of God's handiwork, like a giant overlooking a pigmy, without anything to distinguish it from its surroundings, except its own magnificence. Well, that is enough.

But at this rate we will never get into that "infernal spell of weather" we are seeking. Up the gorge on the right, toward the summit, an ominous cloud begins to creep upon the blue, and we begin to think the prophet will, after all, command respect, but are doomed to disappointment. As the black mass rises over the summit we notice a rift in its center, soon it widens, goes to the right and left, the blue expands, and we are not deprived of a minute's sunshine. We look down into the gorge and see the beautiful stream dancing through the firs, so far below its breadth is shrunk to a handspan, looking now like an emerald ribbon flecked with white, and its rude noise dies into a gentle murmur as a turn in the road shuts it out from sight. On and up; disappointed about the storm nearing the summit, reaching out for the snow and the Alpine primrose, gorgeous in crimson and royal purple; finding the flowers, but the snow, alas that has been gone this three weeks, except a dirt-begrimed bushel or so a few rods from the station.

It is high noon, and, for the first time, I stand upon the "backbone of the continent," and a good deal of a backbone it is, here only eleven thousand four hundred and odd feet high. There must have been trouble in the neighborhood when the continent got its back up to this extent; the agitation experienced in the framing and signing of the Declaration of Independence was evidently trifling in comparison. I did not look down into the Pacific, but saw where the waters start that go that way. Never having seen any of them before, I took a mouthful, and from my recollection of those on the Atlantic side I thought I detected a resemblance. The mercury stood at 55° and we had lunch, taken with a healthy appetite sharpened by a three mile walk in the pure light air. Among the grand mountains of the snowy range to the north, I thought I recognized at least one familiar peak, but there was considerable difference of opinion in the party, including Gaskill, the only resident on the summit. This lack of absolute certainty struck me as a little extraordinary, because everybody is usually filled with correct information, and a mountaineer by instinct; I sighed for a tenderfoot.

Lunch concluded, we continued on our way. About three miles by the road, down the western slope, a pretty mountain brook comes tumbling down from the range, and on the bank, surrounded by wildflowers, I noticed an oblong heap of stones — the rude monument of an unfortunate Swede who perished nearby early in the spring of the previous year. Frank, our driver, told us how the ill-fated Norseman had started with a companion from Billy Cozzens' at the head of the Park. They carried nothing save their blankets slung over their shoulders. It was afternoon, and they had "struck out" for the summit, but were met by a blinding storm; how they succeeded in making their way to within a couple of miles of their destination and safety, when the unfortunate, exhausted and discouraged, sank down into the huge drifts and to sleep; how the other, stronger and more resolute, yet powerless to arouse his dying friend, floundered back to a deserted cabin, built a fire and kept himself from freezing, unable to procure assistance till the following day. But when the news reached Cozzens' there was no lack of quick and experienced effort, though they felt, those strong hearts, as they labored on and up through the great masses of snow, that they were going not to the rescue of a life. They hoped he might have been wise and strong enough to burrow into the drifts, but they found him with one arm clasping a small dead pine, just where his companion had left him, covered partly by the white mantle that had proved his death and his winding sheet. They who loved him best would not have selected a more inviting spot for his sepulture than did those strangers.

From this Frank drifted off to an adventure of his own and his cousin Glenn, on this same range, a few winters before. They were both mere boys, of sixteen and eighteen, "shoeing it," each with a light pack, and determined to make the head of the Park before sundown. With the mercury rapidly going down with the sun, the lads started cheerfully over the crust and had got near the spot where the cabin was built, when, by some accident, one of Frank's shoes snapped in two, and he plunged into the drift. The loss of a snowshoe at such a time and place was a mishap that was by no means trivial. It was simply impossible to go on; to remain, of course, was almost certain death. The boys set their wits to work, without shedding any tears. Fortunately, one of them had several balls of sacking twine, which he had bought and was carrying into the Park. Upon that slender thread hung the safety of one at least. Frank laid down on the snow, to get as much surface as possible upon the treacherous crust, and held on to the end of the string while his cousin went on till it was all paid out. Then the cousin slipped off the shoes, tied them to his end, Frank drew them up to himself, got on them, went on down past his cousin, leaving him an end of the line. When he reached his limit, he slipped off the shoes in turn, the cousin hauled them up, and so alternating, they worked their way down to the foot of the range, where the trail was partly broken.

"You bet, I was glad to see that trail," he concluded, with a smile that had something serious in it.

On down the glorious mountain road we make our way at a lively trot, marking the increase in the volume of the Frazier as the range is left behind. After descending some four thousand feet or more, we enter upon an avenue over a mile in length, straight as an engineer can run a line, and adorned on either side with stately pines that keep off the heat. At the other end we discern the comfortable cabin of Cozzens, and as we emerge from the shelter of the trees the head of the Park is spread out into a broad valley before us, guarded by low-lying hills, while here and there against the clear blue sky looms up an occasional snow-capped peak. Bright colors everywhere—the green of the meadow and the darker shade of the pine, the silver-lined leaf of the white-trunked aspen, and flowers countless as the stars, reposing tranquilly under the slanting rays of the afternoon sun. A picture to defy the skill of the artist, but to fill him with admiration.

We must remain overnight, of course, because the team needs a rest, and the twenty odd miles to our destination will be an easy day's drive for the morrow. And to stop means fresh trout for supper and breakfast, with nice cream in the coffee, helped out with light bread and sweet butter; perhaps an elk steak, or a titbit from a mule deer cooked to a turn—"a righteous man regardeth the life of his beast." Besides the fortieth parallel is to be crossed, before we reach the Springs, and the magnificence of that must be reserved for daylight inspection.

Fisherman's Luck

THE distance between Cozzens' and Hot Sulphur Springs was accomplished without accident, and in time for dinner. Camp made, the Springs, in which my comrade, the Doctor, took much interest, were inspected. The curative properties of the waters have been much talked of and written about, but not overestimated; they are helpful and invigorating for the invalid, and a source of gratification, if not a novelty, to the pleasureseeker. The Indians hold them in great veneration; this of itself is a recommendation, for, as a rule, the Ute has no liking for water. The Doctor labored under the impression that I needed a bath; a hot bath, and said so unequivocally; besides, not to take a bath, even if the bath took your hide, would be a violation of the sacred rule of the place, and subject one to the charge of eccentricity. I do not fancy eccentric people nor enthusiastic folk; beside, every acquaintance I might meet would be sure to exclaim with marked astonishment: "What! didn't take a bath!" The thing would become monotonous. I consented to take the bath.

The Doctor went ahead like one accustomed to the treatment. It was night; the place was provided with a single lamp that made the darkness unearthly; the fumes of the sulphur were strong and suggestive; I looked down into the steaming pool with the trepidation that must come over a sinner in the heat of an orthodox revival. The Doctor waded out like a minister at the ordinance of baptism, and called to me to "come down." I said I was coming. I went. The steps were very firm, clean and provided with a strong rail, but I didn't hurry. I put one foot in and took it out right away; when I found it was not raw I put it back, and concluded as the Doctor was not yet parboiled I might put in the other foot; but I did not go in a foot at a time, only about an inch. Then I asked the Doctor what church he belonged to, and started to go out when he said he was a Methodist. I sat down on the steps, inhaled the sulphur and looked at him floundering round in that pool like a school of porpoises out at sea. He told me to try it again. I said I was sleepy and wanted to go to bed. Then he said it would make my hair grow, and I told him I didn't want any hair, that I had had it pulled out on purpose before I was married. Then he said it would make me fat; I told him I was dieting to take off superfluous flesh. Then he said he would tell what he insinuated was generally suspected, that I was afraid of water; I told him I didn't care. Finally he swore that if I did not get off that perch and come down into the bath, he'd destroy the commissaries and refuse to show me any of the trout pools in the Park. I was inspired to say I'd try it again; he had been there five minutes at least and was not cooked, and if he could stand it that long with his religious training, I thought I might venture on as many seconds. But I made haste slowly, got in by degrees and laid down. Then the Doctor got under the "shower bath," where the water tumbles, six feet or more in a great stream, into the pool; he wanted me to try that. But I told him I was very well satisfied where I was, and that I did not approve of shower baths, anyway; then I went on to explain to him the deleterious effects of too much bathing, and of shower baths in particular. I talked to him as well as I could for ten minutes, sitting the while upon the bottom of the pool with the water up to my chin; but he would not be convinced. I think the situation and the noise of the waterfall may have detracted somewhat from the force of my argument. The Doctor said it was time to get out, but having become warmed up on the subject, I deemed this a mere evasion, and told him not to hurry; that I could convince him of the correctness of my theory inside a half hour. He said he had no doubt of it if I remained where I was for that length of time. He had, to some extent, won my confidence; by his combined advice and threats he had enabled me to realize an ideal, and at the same time be in the fashion, and this not in the days of miracles. When I got out of that bath I felt as I have heard men say they felt after a hard day's work. I took my blankets, laid on the ground and slept the sleep of godliness. Some of those fellows whose consciences are demoralized had better try this medicine instead of opium; it is at least a safer narcotic. One can go to bed with better assurance that in a day or so a servant will not be peering over the transom and finding a subject for the coroner. It is more satisfactory, too, in such emergencies, in that it removes the doubts of friends, if one has any, as well as of the public, as to "the cause," and entitles one to Christian burial.

Awakened the next day by that invaluable servant to us all shining in my face, I reminded the Doctor of his promise concerning the trout pools. So we were up betimes, had breakfast, the horses saddled, and with creels capable of fourteen pounds each and a stock of tackle sufficient to start a store, we were off across the Grand, and over the hills for the anticipated pleasure downstream, to a place where the Doctor was sure no one had been. The horses of tourists and amateur fishermen usually buck and raise the devil when starting out on such a jaunt, and I was disappointed that the Doctor's animal did not bow his back, go up, and come down stiff-legged. I like to see a horse buck when somebody else is on him, and I like to hear the man pray, if he is able, when he feels the ground and glances round to see who is laughing at him. An even-tempered gentleman like the Doctor would have afforded an enviable example of Christian fortitude under such circumstances—his horse did not buck, but led the way over the hills as quietly as a cow going out to pasture.

We kept away from the river, traveled over high ground, and through an upland of black sagebrush that would rival the mesa between Pueblo and Cañon. We followed an Indian trail, and followed it so long that I began to inquire when we were to reach my much coveted destination. The Doctor called my attention to a belt of timber some distance ahead, and said we were "going up there." I asked him if he expected that trout roosted like sage hens, and informed him that if such had been his experience, it had not been mine, and that I was going to find water. He told me to do as I pleased, so I struck off toward the Grand—I like to be independent sometimes. My horse went scrambling through the thick sagebrush, catching his toes in the roots and threatening to throw me over his head every few minutes, until finally he stopped at the bank of the river. It was fifty feet, at least, down to the water. I looked up stream half a mile, then down to the belt of timber, and that same bank presented itself at an aggravating angle of about ninety degrees. I don't like Indians, nor any of their belongings, as a general rule, but I went cheerfully back to that trail, and quietly followed in the Doctor's wake. When I caught up, the Doctor said in a mild sort of way that it was generally safe to keep on the trail. We walked our horses to the timber and into it, the Doctor in the lead. We got about half way round the mountain with a thousand or fifteen hundred feet of earth, rocks and trees below us, and as many above, when the Doctor discovered a "cut-off." He led the way for a few rods, when a tree about three feet in diameter barred further progress in that direction. We could not turn round, nor could we go on, so we got off, and persuaded the horses to climb perpendicularly fifty feet up to the trail. I was satisfied in my mind that the Doctor was more than ever convinced of the safety of keeping on the trail, but he did not say so to me.

We kept on to Williams' Fork, and picketed our horses about half a mile from the mouth. The Doctor then proposed that we "hoof it" over more hills. I began to be disgusted, but was away from home and at the mercy of this new-fangled fisherman. I didn't know an Indian trail from a cow path, and was as likely to get into one as the other. A trail, like the road of a civilized brother, leads to some place, but a cow path —. I puffed on behind, up a high ridge of rocks, and as soon as I could get the breath, told the Doctor I was obliged to him. We stood upon a Grand Canyon in miniature. I want to describe it, but I can't. After dreaming over it awhile, the Doctor told me an incident in his experience concerning the ledge where we had precarious foothold, looking down into the seething waters several hundred feet below. The Doctor, Wm. H. Beard, the artist, Bayard Taylor and a prospector and mining man came over the trail a few years before on horseback, the Doctor in the lead, then the prospector, and, finally, the artist and the great traveler bringing up the rear. When the prospector passed the narrow ledge, barely sufficient in width to allow a horseman to squeeze along, where one has to hang, as it were, like a fly on a wall, he became conscious that his saddle girths needed tightening. With the recklessness peculiar to his craft, he slipped off his mule, and was engaged in the necessary adjustment of his bellyband when Beard reached the narrow ledge and had to stop. The first intimation the Doctor had of anything wrong came in the way of an emphatic adjuration, that might have been heard half a mile, for the blessed prospector to get out of that. The Doctor said he was glad the artist was not given to profanity, though he said a great deal to the miner that the Doctor could not understand; it did not sound like English nor Dutch, nor any language the Doctor had ever heard, but hurled at the head of the miner from a two-foot trail hanging over five or six hundred feet of perpendicular granite, it seemed to have an accelerating effect. The miner led his mule to more convenient quarters without finishing his task, and the artist followed, not in silence, however; he did not seem to be able to get through his business with that miner for an hour.

Looking down into the chasm, I suggested that it did not seem particularly "pokerish." The Doctor said it was well enough to say so when one was afoot, "but just try it horseback," in that ambiguous sort of way that always rouses one's determination to undertake it. I did a few days after, but in returning I led my horse.

Getting through with his anecdote, the Doctor pointed to another pile of rocks half a mile further up the stream, and called my especial attention to a pool beneath, which, even at that distance, placed me under conviction that I could see trout therein, two feet long at least. I started to get some of them. Arrived there, we shipped our tackle, and I selected a spot under a pinetree on one side of this pregnant pool, while the Doctor took the other. I made a cast with an anxiety indescribable; I knew I would have the first strike, and I did; the fly caught in the luxuriant foliage overhead. I tried to coax the blasted thing loose, but the more I prayed and persuaded the more obstinately the line interlaced itself. If there is anything more exasperating than to get a line fastened in a pinetree, I want to know what it is; a "picked-up dinner" on wash day is bliss in comparison. Not being able to untangle the line, I tried to pull down the tree; then I took a seat on the bank and patiently renewed my leader. Meanwhile the Doctor was threshing the peaceful waters industriously. I asked him if he had caught anything; he said he was going to very soon, and threshed away. When I got my line fixed I murmured, "but deliver us from evil," and got out of the reach of that pine, when I labored faithfully for full fifteen minutes, till finally we scared up a trout about six inches long. He came browsing around with his head half out of water and an inquiring expression plainly visible in his bright eyes, then he disappeared wiggling his tail in derision. We worked away in hope of bringing the scaly monster once more to the surface. A second sight of him would have been comforting; but his curiosity was evidently satisfied. I asked the Doctor if this was one of the trout pools he had been bragging about, and he said it was; he had always caught trout out of that hole, and the stories he told me of the numbers he had lifted out of that place "in the short space of an hour," were marvelous. While listening and trying to believe him I felt a sudden jerk at my rod. Up to that moment I had entertained no special antipathy to stop-reels. But with one leader unattainable in the profuse growth overhead, and another serving as a sort of submarine union jack to an unknown denizen of the pool, with no prospect of satisfaction, I felt—not like Patience. The trout must have been a monster, of course, or he never would have snapped that gut with so little ceremony. I shall not soon forget the sensation; it was a single and sudden blow without pause for a second pull, as though his troutship in passing that way had snapped up that fly and gone on about his business or pleasure, without realizing in the remotest degree that he had done anything more than take a midge floating on the surface of his habitation. To avoid a repetition of the calamity, I cheerfully tied the check to a crossbar of the reel, looped on another leader, and resumed, with an angler's vow registered in heaven, which I have religiously kept.

With that commendable resignation born of experience, I worked that pool for half an hour, gave up in disgust and started downstream—the Doctor followed in humiliation. We whipped every foot of the way down through the cañon to our horses, but not a fin rewarded our efforts. The forenoon was gone; I felt sorry for the Doctor; my sympathies went out to him as they always do for the underdog in the fight. I had no heart to express anything but unbounded satisfaction for the morning's enjoyment. But I believe he thinks to this day I was lying.

Agapae

DID you never go fishing when a boy, and come home at the close of a Saturday without so much as a single chub dangling on a string to console you for the anticipated dressing because of your interdicted absence? I have. But the chagrin of the ten-year-old is nothing in comparison to the mortification of the middle-aged boy under similar circumstances. However, there were no inquisitive bores in our camp. The Doctor was determined to again try his luck in Williams' Fork; nothing but the remembrance of my early experience could have induced me to join him.

The day after our successful failure, equipped as before, we took our way over the hills and through the sagebrush, reaching our destination about nine o'clock. The tackle was quickly adjusted, and keeping out of the way of that infernal pine, I dropped a brown-bodied gray hackle gently upon the placid water. The fly had hardly touched the surface, when suddenly from out of the depths there flashed an open-mouthed beauty, and that hackle disappeared as, turning head down and revealing his glittering side, its captor plunged again into the till then silent pool. It made my pulse throb a little quicker, but I was not paying as much attention to that as to the trout. He made a dart upstream with the hook firmly fixed; I brought him gradually round and coaxed him to the surface to ascertain what sort of a leviathan I had encountered; then I got excited and felt that if I did not get him ashore very soon he was not my trout. Just below the pool, ten yards or so, was a shelving beach a few feet in length, and I gradually worked my way to it, keeping a taut line on my bonanza. While I was doing this I remembered having read a whole column of imagination, written by somebody named Murray, wherein he described his "happiness" under like circumstances; cracking bamboo and spinning silk, with a half dozen Johns with landing nets, were the burden of his effusion, and he wound the matter up after a three hours' fight, with a trout seventeen inches long, when I expected to learn at least of a ten-pound salmon lifted out by one of the Johns above mentioned. I wanted to hit the fellow with a club for making an ass of himself. I was hungry for trout, and inside five minutes I had drawn my prize up to and on that gravelly beach, had him by the gills, and he was seventeen inches flush, big as

Mr. Murray's and no fuss about it. Just as I got my fish secured I heard the Doctor threshing round in the willows, about two rods away, and in a moment after he held up to my envious gaze more than a match for my capture. Our exchange of congratulations was hurried; the Doctor cast in his hopper; I stuck to the gray hackle, and inside half an hour I had landed a dozen good-sized trout, and the Doctor had "yanked out" as many more. The pool and the Doctor were redeemed; we had not quite "fished it out," had only taken those with sharp appetites. But that kind of success demoralizes one for the time being, so we moved off down the creek, trying the eddies and below the riffles; now and again dropping the fly under the lee of the larger boulders in midstream, with varying success, until we reached our horses. Our creels were full enough to carry with comfort and we started for camp, discussing the causes of the failure of the day before, but arriving at no satisfactory solution.

The rapidity with which news of success in trouting will travel through the various camps in one's vicinity is somewhat singular, and is only equaled by the celerity with which the reports of the quantity captured is multiplied. Having more than we could consume, we gave some to our nearest neighbor, who came over to see our catch. We learned the next day that we had caught anywhere from twenty-five pounds to a hundred, and I am unable to say how many went exploring for trout on the day following. That some were unsuccessful I know, because several swore to me that there was not even a minnow in Williams' Fork. There was one young gentleman in particular who appealed to me in a tone of remonstrance after a day spent in unsuccessful labor down the Grand. He was dressed in light drab pants, cheviot shirt, and a broad-brimmed felt hat, the band of which was stuck full of flies of all sizes and a multitude of colors. He had a fifty-dollar rod and a fifteen-dollar reel of wonderful combination; his eyes, emphatic with disgust, glaring through his glasses, he avowed there were no fish in the Park. He held up a crimson fly that would have driven crazy any fish except a sucker, and would have scared a sucker if sunk to his level, and wanted to know of me if I didn't think it a fine fly. I told him I did. He said he had whipped five miles of water with that fly and could not get a rise. I told him that the trout was a queer fish, and that perhaps he had better try a blue flannel rag, and offered to give him a piece of my shirt, but he got mad, tore around, and threatened, in popular parlance, to take off the top of my head. Believing this to be a more painful operation than scalping, I apologized, and the difficulty was promptly adjusted. Then I gave him a gray hackle and told him that that was to the trout what bread was to civilized man, a staple article of which he seldom grew tired, or if he did, to try the brown hackle, which, still like the bread, was a wholesome change; that if he could get neither the gray nor the brown, then to take a grasshopper, pull off his legs and wings, and string it upon a number six Kirby; that such a hook would take a three ounce or a three pound trout with equal facility.

The next evening I saw my new acquaintance; his drab pants were ruined, his rod had been shivered into kindling wood, his reel lay in a pool of the Grand twenty feet deep. He had cast that gray hackle with a brown body into that pool; it had been seized upon by a trout something "near a yard long"; the angler had succeeded in landing its head upon the rocks, then his rod gave way and he fell on the fish, rolled into the river, lost the remains of his tackle and his hat with the flies, and some other tenderfoot who happened providentially that way, had pulled him out by the collar. He was happy, and said he would write to his mother, for which I commended him. This morning I saw him following a trail down the Grand; he had provided himself with some hackles and had a pole cut from a plum bush. I predicted for him success or a watery grave.

In tender consideration of the tyro in these waters, I may be permitted to make a few suggestions as to tackle, based upon my own experience. In the matter of lures the taste of the trout must be considered; as to all else you may consult your own. It is well to have in your fly books a *little* of everything, but of gray and brown hackles, as already intimated, coachmen and professors, an abundance. The best reel is one that combines lightness and durability, and is incapable of fouling your line, no matter how negligent you may be; a click reel of hard rubber and metal, with a revolving disk, the handle fixed upon the outer edge, and weighing, with thirty yards of line, about five ounces, will answer well. For lines there is, to my mind, nothing equal to the braided and tapered waterproof silk (size F); being the best, they are the cheapest, easily managed, and less liable to snarl or call for a tax upon your patience. For a rod always select one of three joints; they hang more evenly and have a "better feel." Ash butt and second joint, with lancewood tip; Greenheart or Bethabara; try any and all; break them on the least provocation, which means a ten-inch trout or less, but wreck two or three by the "yanking process," or otherwise. Then, when you feel that you can handle a rod with the same deftness a mother her firstborn, save up your money and buy a first class split bamboo. When you get it have faith in it, for if properly made it will bend, if necessity demands, till the tip touches the butt, yet do not needlessly try that conclusion with it; neither must you attempt to lift your fish out of the water with it. When you have fairly exhausted your trout, take the line in your disengaged hand; there are moments between struggles when you can swing your catch safely to land, without a movement on his part; when he will come out as straight as the plumb line Amos saw. If in his struggles his troutship should clear the water, something I never saw a trout do, bow the rod to him, of course, as he returns, so that he may not get his unsupported weight upon the beautiful toy. Keep a taut line upon your prey—by this I do not mean that you should give him no line, but let the strain be steady, giving only when you must. After the first few rushes, you may generally with safety press your thumb upon the line, and let him feel the spring of your rod; that will kill him quickly. The climax in the poem of trouting is the spring of the split bamboo. In striking, remember you have not a plum bush sapling and that it is not incumbent upon you to bail the stream with an artificial fly; let it be done with a quick motion of the wrist; a motion which, if you should miss the game, would move your fly but a little way. If your catch is too large to lift out as I have suggested, in the absence of a landing net, you can generally find a place, always downstream, where you can safely, if you go about it gently, snake him out, or get your finger under his gills. Much more might be written, and what I have said is by no means new, but the purpose is to put you in the way merely of avoiding the calamity that befell the tackle of my acquaintance in the drab pants. Have a taste for the sport, "let your own discretion be your tutor," and you will work out your own salvation more surely than by a library of directions, remembering this for an axiom, that: The true sportsman does not go downstream and afield for the mere love of killing something.

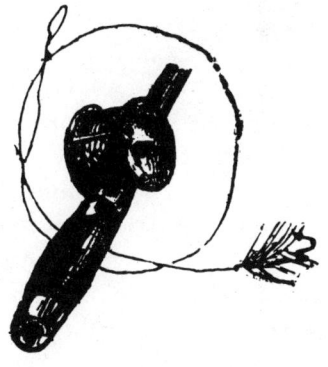

Black Lake in 1878

TWO or three years since, a couple of divines, imbued, doubtless, with a spirit of adventure, found their way up one of the tributaries of the Blue. They discovered a lake nestled away in the grand old hills, and in about the last place one would think of looking for a lake. They called it Black Lake, very appropriately, and when they made known their discovery there were found some of those disagreeable two-legged animals who are never surprised at anything, and who knew, of course, that "the lake had been there all the time." The ministers, however, took away with them the credit of the discovery, though but few people manifested any interest in the matter. As a result of the indifference, the merits of the lake have been but little talked about, and when mentioned at all, it has been treated with a sort of indefiniteness, as a place that had been heard of, but was not known, except that it was "up there, somewhere," in the rugged range of the Blue. One was, and is, also, always reminded by the would-be informant that "a couple of preachers found it," in that particular sort of tone that at once conveys the impression that, because a preacher was instrumental in making the discovery, it must be a kind of slough of despond, or an eight-by-ten water hole, or a beaver pond, with a few decayed water lilies mourning round the margin. It may be that there is much skepticism hereaway concerning the general level-headedness of gentlemen in orders, where our mountain scenery is involved. Your "rugged frontiersman"—to whom these grandeurs are every-day affairs, still new everyday, and not the less revered—worships in silence, and is apt to think your enthusiast off his tender feet the moment he opens his mouth. "There is no use trying to do the subject justice by attempting to describe what you see. Just look about you, realize that you are not the greatest thing in creation, and, with a chastened spirit, go tell your friends to come and see and worship." So your gentlemen in flannel shirt and foxed breeches would recommend, and they mean well. But if enthusiasm is pardonable at all, it may be overlooked in a man fresh from his books and his daily, dull routine, suddenly set down in the midst of such evidences of God's handiwork as one finds here. The ordained discoverers of Black Lake did not, evidently, adopt the reticent method of expressing their veneration for the grand surroundings, and their delight at the beautiful lake so unexpectedly revealed to them. They were unquestionably very enthusiastic, and consequently more the object of doubt. If they had said simply: "We found a lake up there, just under the base of that cone-shaped peak," and pointed out the mountain, there would have been a dozen visitors to the spot before the end of the summer. Your pioneer would have told it that way, and that would have been notoriety. As it was, Grand Lake, the Twin Lakes, and other known lakes in the mountains made Black Lake a possibility. A few have taken the trouble to go in search of it, the Doctor, who is no tenderfoot, and myself, a little younger, among the number.

The trip determined upon, the next step was to make preparation. The experience of my indefatigable Mentor enabled him to speedily devise all plans and complete them. A pack animal was at once forthcoming, and upon it were secured four days' provisions, a coffee pot, frying pan, two tin cups, a pair of blankets and a rubber poncho; the limited number of utensils inculcating a lesson in economy—a practical illustration of what we need and what we think we must possess to be happy. With our four days lares and penates thus secured and armed with our fishing tackle, a bright August morning saw us in the saddle and on the road.

The first few miles of our route were by the Indian trail, already familiar as far as Williams' Fork, thence up the long mesa bordering that stream, toward Ute Mountain. Bands of antelope frequently starting up and scampering away refuted the insinuation of another young gentleman in glasses and lavender pants who had been hunting up and down the high roads for a week, within half a mile of the Springs, and "couldn't find any game in the Park." The same young gentleman told me that he had seen what he understood to be sage hens, but could not kill them with a rifle—he must have something larger—and then wanted to know of me if there were no "sage roosters." I told him there were, lots of 'em; that they were web-footed, had ruffles round their necks and wore lavender-colored legs at this season; whereat he expressed himself satisfied and said he would find one. I expect to see him chased into camp some day by a mountain woodchuck—then we'll have another bear story. While I am writing this, that same young man is fishing in the Grand in sight of my tent; he has waded out and is standing knee-deep, whipping the stream just where a hot sulphur spring bubbles up throwing the steam above the surface. He, too, has a valuable rod. I wish he had to stay there enjoying his homeopathic sulphur bath till the fellow with the club could come along and kill him.

Looking round after the antelope resulted in

our losing the trail. We started in the direction to cross it, but, with the exasperating contrariness peculiar to the country, traveled parallel with it for more than a mile, and until we ran into a body of timber which the Doctor knew the trail had nothing to do with. Then we struck off at right angles. I told the Doctor that he was heading for camp; he said he intended to make camp about six o'clock. I urged him not to be discouraged, that we might yet reach our destination, and that I did not like to be disappointed. But he trotted on, in silence, found the trail within two hundred yards and turned into it. By this time I did not know Ute Mountain from Gray's Peak. We jogged on to the timber clothing the hills on the north side of Ute Pass, crossed a little brook, left a blind trail to the right, recrossed the brook, and in about five minutes we were playing circus among a lot of fallen timber, with no more sign of a trail in sight than there was a prospect of our getting out of the blasted place inside a week. Had the devil been really a man of genius, instead of covering Job with boils, destroying his flocks and killing his relatives, he would some forenoon have inveigled that much abused patriarch up a steep mountainside and deposited him in about forty acres of fallen timber. Then when Job's dinner hour came round he would have tried to get out of that, and after about ten minutes of that kind of pastime he would have begun to realize that old Mrs. Job would be looking for him with the same kind of disposition they keep dinner waiting for us in these days. Just then the devil would have gained his point.

I ventured to ask the Doctor, while he and his horse were crawling through a symmetrical masterpiece of accidental log architecture, if he knew where the trail was. I was deferential, knowing the subject of trails was to him a delicate one. He said, of course, he knew where it was; on the other side of the brook. Encouraged by his affability, I then inquired why he had left it; he said there were some rough places ahead of us, and that he wanted to drill the horses a little before we reached them. Then I asked him if he didn't think we had better go back to the Springs and give me an opportunity to employ a broncho breaker to drill my horse; he said if I did not break my dashed neck before I got out of that I might do so. All this time I was trying to follow him round, between, under and over dead trees, wondering what sort of battle-field was in store for me if this was only a parade ground. We finally, deployed by a perpendicular-horizontal-right-and-left-oblique, gained the other side of the brook and the trail. Then the Doctor said that we were all right, in a tone that carried conviction.

We jogged on, uphill and down, through timbered land and little meadows, by the sides of deep gorges and under huge cliffs, now in the sunlight and again through such dense forests of heavy firs that night seemed to have set in, until we reached the summit of the Pass, and looked beyond upon the massive and frowning Blue River range, riven in mighty fissures, its sharp peaks kissing the azure sky, its great gorges filled with the eternal snows, now rosy under the rays of the setting sun, and over all brooding a solemn stillness that bade the heart bow in humility and reverential awe. In such a presence if a man does not realize his own utter insignificance, he is justified in believing that "all things are created for him," even office. Toiling slowly down, we reached the Blue, now, however, yellow with the work of the gold hunter, crossed it, and made camp before dark. After supper, and tired with our day's ride, we spread our blankets under the great roof fretted with golden fire, and slept the sleep of the weary.

The sun was scarcely out of bed next morning before we were astir and on the road to Roaring Fork. A boistrous name, truly, and indicating nearly five miles of cascade. Since the discovery of the lake it is sometimes called Black Lake Creek, but the noisy name is more apt. Crossing the Fork we followed up the right bank, without any trail, for about four miles, at which point we deemed it advisable to camp, picket our horses and proceed on foot. We reached the lake after a tiresome climb of a few hundred yards, afterwards, of course, discovering a much easier route from our camp, and over which we might have ridden the horses to our destination.

The lake is about a mile by three-quarters in size, a narrow point jutting out at the foot giving it somewhat the shape of a crescent. Along the margin, when the lake is perfectly calm, the bottom seems to shelve to irregular distances, when the light color of the crystal water suddenly changes to a hue almost black, at once suggestive of precipitous and tremendous depths, and which, no doubt, prompted the giving of its name. To the left, its base lapped by this gem of the mountains, rises a cone-shaped spur of the range with summit far above timberline, and its rugged clefts filled with snow. In front of you the main range, seemingly lower only because more distant, with rocky, snow-crowned heads overtopping the velvety-looking firs that reach down to the western margin; and from out the dense foliage coming and receding upon the pure air is the music of falling waters. For there is hidden there a beautiful fall, with its source far away in front of you in those great snowfields; in one place having a perpendicular descent of fifty feet or more, and in another dashing and tumbling down its precipitous bed over huge boulders for hundreds of feet, like a great artery pouring crystal life and beauty into the little queen below. And on the right, yet another mighty mountain, with verdant base and snow-crowned head, sloping gradually away behind the nearer hills. It must, indeed, have been a revelation and a glad surprise to the man who first discovered it, as it was to us who went not to be surprised, but for another pleasant purpose.

We found on the point of land and down near the water's edge, a shelter of canvass and pine boughs, a Dutch oven, tin cans empty and full, an old pair of boots, some fishing tackle and other evidences of man's presence. Besides there was a boat and a couple of rafts moored to the beach and a fish box anchored a short distance out. We contented ourselves with looking over these desecrations, which had on first view taken nine-tenths of the romance out of the picture, and walked back to camp, intent only upon the quantity of trout we were to take out of the prolific depths.

The first hour's effort after dinner produced only disappointment. I could see nothing of the Caliban of the Point, and was loath to touch his property, feeling that most men under like surroundings are always ready to grant favors and equally quick to resent a liberty. Casting the fly from the shore resulted in only an occasional strike, while all parts of the lake were being aggravatingly broken into circles by the leaping trout. Finally I worked round the point toward the outlet, somewhat disgusted but determined to exhaust all my temptations. The first cast there, with a red-bodied gray hackle, brought an instant rise, and I was kept busy for half an hour, the fish varying but little in size, running from ten to twelve inches. I did not make slow work of my part of the business, and in less than an hour had about eight pounds of the little fellows in my creel. The Doctor had found quarters where equal success had attended him, so far as quantity was concerned, but as usual, he had to catch one fine fellow larger than any I could boast. The bright salmon color of the beauty flashed upon me irritatingly not five rods away as he was seized upon and held up exultantly by my companion.

Satisfied with our afternoon's sport, we returned to camp with the prospect of a wetting from overhead. The clouds continued to thicken; we got supper — coffee, bread and trout. You of Denver, who get trout only in the market, have yet to learn the exquisite flavor of the fish. The first time you eat one, properly prepared, within an hour from the time of his capture, you will wager on your ability to eat trout only, three times a day for a month; believe me, and I am no particular lover of fish diet either, as you may have readily concluded. The rain had not begun yet, and the Doctor, full of resources, had improvised a shelter out of the rubber poncho, and with our blankets spread under it, and a bright campfire to take off the chill of the night air, we realized the comforts of roughing it in genuine style. But it did not rain, and we went to sleep; I maturing ways and means to discover the owner of the property on the Point.

About noon next day I discovered my man, in buckskin, and lost no time in making his acquaintance. We intended to start upon our return trip at four o'clock; as yet, that morning, I had enticed out of the lake barely eight trout, and had but little time left to remunerate myself for a thirty-five mile ride. He said if I would be patient till he got some dinner he would take me out on a raft and teach me to catch trout. I said I was willing to learn, and he asked me to dine with him, which I did, off bread and butter and stewed blackberries with lake water for grog, and I have made worse meals. Then we went down and got on board one of those rafts; it was constructed of four logs each about six inches in diameter and eight feet long, held together by cleats and wooden pins—a rollicking craft to put to sea in. Notwithstanding its questionable appearance, I took my seat on a soap box to which I was invited, and my chaperone seized his paddle and pushed the machine from the shore into deep water. I would rather it had not been so deep, and as I tried to see bottom and couldn't, I thought it would be less disagreeable to drown in ten feet of water than two hundred— your friends could find your precious remains so much easier, and would not be debarred the luxury of a funeral. While there was conviction in the assurance of the captain that "the old thing" was safe, I nevertheless handled myself gingerly. I cast my fly upon the waters with immediate success. The skipper, inspired by my example, dropped his paddle, and attempted competition. After a few minutes of unavailing effort, during which time I had all I could attend to, he looked down at me with a puzzled expression in his gray eyes, and exclaimed:

"Why, Mister, you beat all the men to catch trout I ever see; what kind of fly you got?"

I gave him the infallible gray hackle with the red body; he took it doubtingly, while I bore my honors meekly. After landing half a dozen trout in quick succession, the doubter again broke silence:

"I say, Mister, have you got any of them flies to spare?"

I told him I had, and he was happy.

The Doctor had gone round to the inlet upon our arrival in the morning, and was apparently busy when I started on my voyage. We were about an hour in reaching him, when he informed us that he had all he could carry. My own creel was nearly full, and before we got back to our starting point it was running over, and I dropped the surplus in the fish box with which the raft was provided, that the skipper might be helped, as he was fishing for market, and doing it in a legitimate way.

I had flattered myself that in previous years, in some of our virgin streams, I had enjoyed the sport, but the hour and a half spent upon Black Lake demonstrated that, as to the race against time, my previous seasons had been failures. A man under such circumstances is tempted to make a "trout hog" of himself, and I told my new acquaintance that I'd like to stay with him a week.

"Just fetch your traps right up here, Mister, I'd be mighty glad to have you," was his cordial response. But I was obliged to decline; it was too much of a good thing.

That afternoon the Doctor and I again made our camp on the banks of the Blue. I had had three days of genuine enjoyment, but when I laid down that night the heavens were overcast. We were to experience the felicity of sleeping with the rain pelting on us. I wished for a tent, a tree, a clump of willows, but it was too late; we had made our bed and must lie in it; there was no shelter anywhere, nor even the means to erect the poncho, so we spread it on top of us. When the drops began to fall, I pulled it over my head, and as they came thicker and faster, thought of "The Rain on the Roof," and in about half an hour felt a chill on my weather side, put my hand down to straighten the cover and felt a pool of water. It crept up that side and under me. I told the Doctor of my condition. He said it was nothing; that it would do me good, in fact. I told him I thought I'd get up. He wanted to know where I would go. I said I did not know. Then he advised me to go to sleep. I asked him if he was under water, but he said he was dry as a bone and warm. I offered to change places with him, but he said he was sleepy, and that I had better say my prayers and go to sleep as he was about to do. I thought of all I had heard of the danger of damp sheets, of rheumatisms, fevers—chills I had—colds, and other ills resulting from such exposure; then of the men who had slept that way and lied about the comfort of it; then I wished it was day, and wondered how many hours I would have to lie there; then I felt that Coates Kinney was a fraud, and his "Rain on the Roof" a satire, and registered a vow that if I ever allowed myself to be again caught in such a d—amp fix, I hoped some fellow would hit me with a club; then I went to sleep, and awoke at sunrise. I would have had no reluctance in moving about had my clothes been dry, but the sensation to me of the clinging garments was—well, we kindled a fire; I got a cup of hot coffee under my waistband and felt better, and have been feeling better ever since. We reached the Springs about four o'clock, tired, of course, but with the memory of a four days' jaunt to look back upon that half-a-dozen rainstorms could not wash out.

Egotism and — Rods

WRITER in *The Angler*, I think, apologized for giving his personal experiences, in that they savored of egotism. To my mind he should not have done so. What a world this would be if every man kept his personal experience to himself.

Egotism may not perhaps be a cardinal virtue; but good may come out of Nazareth. One's personal experiences are more novel than romances; the egotist need not necessarily be a follower of Des Cartes. If my egotism affords a brother a few moments' pleasure, or he is in any way profited, then my life has not been a total failure.

Then, again, what is the use of apologizing for an universal weakness. If we do not talk about ourselves, we are always tickled to have others talk of us, and many would rather be abused than not be noticed at all. Doubtless vanity and egotism are at the bottom of most of the good things of this life, just as discontent is the father of perfected things.

De Quincey would make a martyr of Judas; looked at from the De Quincey standpoint, Judas was a broad-gauged man. If so eminent a scholar may make a nobleman out of the King of Traitors, as we have been taught to regard him, certainly one, even so poor as I, may take up the cudgels in defense of mine own and my brother's folly. I flatter myself, too, that I should be more successful in carrying conviction than the learned author of "murder considered as a fine art." He combated a prejudice; I should tickle the tender side of nine out of ten—if the nine would only confess.

The pronoun I is the straightest letter in the alphabet; the only one independent of curves or angles for support; for this reason it is entitled to every man's respect.

But I do not intend to enter into a defense of egotism at this writing; this is only to express a willingness to enter the lists should occasion demand, and to admonish the man who would deprecate egotism that he himself is full of that commendable weakness. I wish to give my experience, a very limited one, with rods.

An immediate change from a three pound plum bush pole to an aesthetic split bamboo rod of a few ounces would drive a man crazy. It would be like putting a delicately turned Kirby into the hands of a pot hunter of the stone age. As the Kirby would compare with a bone sharpened at the ends, and a hole in the middle for the rawhide line, so the little bamboo with the plum bush. No doubt the prehistoric angler and his descendant of the nineteenth century would look, if they could, each upon the implements of the other with curiosity and utter lack of faith. But faith comes with education, and when the labor of learning is a labor of love, education becomes easy.

My experience with the plum bush was not satisfactory. Early in the "sixties," depending on ox teams for bacon and flour, fishing rods were not counted as merchandise or articles of freight. Necessity therefore required, that, to indulge my liking, I must exert my skill, so that when I got back from Bear Creek and my memorable first trouting, I made a rod; my first rod.

A piece of pine for the butt, cedar, straight grained and without flaw, for the second joint. A well selected hickory whip handle furnished the timber for a tip. A jackknife, glass and sandpaper served for tools; and excellent tools they are with patience for capital.

I shall not say how many days I exhausted in working up those three sticks into satisfactory shape.

As to mounting, I had neither tools nor metal, nor the genius of Tubal Cain, so I applied to a tinker of watches, made known my difficulty, and he fitted me out with two sets of ferrules and half a dozen guide rings for the modest sum of seven dollars in gold dust.

Drugstores and whisky shops get to the frontier with equal facility, so there was no scarcity of oil, shellac and alcohol. The wrapping of the rings was followed by the oil and shellac, and when I strung that rod together, and, in the privacy of our cabin, submitted it to the inspection of the madam, it was pronounced "just perfect."

The verdict was no less delightful than the rod and the jury of one.

During the winter that marvel of excellence and beauty was subjected to weekly examinations and comment. The anticipated pleasures of the coming summer, because we were "both going," were the prime subjects of evening conversations over the kitchen stove. There never had been, nor could there ever be, vouchsafed to any other couple the amount of enjoyment banked up and ready to draw upon, than was stored away during that memorable winter, and the rod was the polestar, so to speak. Everything pointed to that. But disappointments make life worth living; while they are sometimes severe, there is yet a genuine pleasure in setting one's foot on their necks.

I never flourished my masterpiece of mechanical skill over anything save the weeds and the few straggling vegetables that decorated our backyard.

The rod was too good to keep. I lost it early, just as the good children die.

I had, and yet have, a friend, whom I'll call Sam, because that is his name. About a month before the time fixed for our departure to the hills, Sam came over and told me I had a fishing rod, as though I had been the only man in town unacquainted with the fact. He said he wanted to borrow it for a few days, he wanted to go fishing and hoped I'd accommodate him! Think of loaning your watch to a two-year-old for a day or so. He promised, of course, to bring it back in good order; I expected no less—than the promise, I mean, and cheerfully allowed him to walk off with it. I never saw it again, but I am glad to say I saw Sam. He came back in about a week; there was nothing the matter with him, his bones were whole, he hadn't got drowned, nor been bitten by rattlesnakes, nor chased by bears, nor clawed by mountain lions, nor lost his scalp. The mosquitoes had been a little troublesome; there was some comfort in that, but not enough to speak of. He had come over to see me; he said, about "that fishing rod."

"Yes, the fact is, I found an old friend on South Boulder, and he took such a fancy to that rod, that I could do no less than make him a present of it. It's a splendid rod, that's a fact, and I don't know exactly how I can replace it, just now; I'm sorry you're disappointed at my not returning it, but I don't see—"

We were not a very ceremonious community in those days, though kindly disposed. At the outset I was on the point of telling Sam to say his shortest prayer, if he had more than one, but changed my mind and told him not to say anymore about it. It was some time before he would be convinced that I was not mad.

That summer I fished with a clear conscience and a plum bush pole and had a good time.

By the time the season was over Sam came round again. He brought with him a rod; it had four joints and an extra tip; it was of ash and lance wood. Sam had sent to the states for the treasure by ox team, and had ordered a reel in addition. These he informally turned over to me, still doubtful of my condition of mind. I tried to make him understand that from the first I had felt that his love for me had prompted him to treat my property as his own. He finally caught the idea, and the first trout I caught on that rod was twenty inches long.

I have the rod yet, with one of the original tips; I have used it every summer since; if no accident happens it may last forever. A few years since I changed the reel seat, put the whole concern through a whip-wrapping machine, and think I have improved it. I have never weighed it, and I do not intend to say how many pounds of trout it has been fatal to. In accordance with the frontier rule, "she" has a name: "the old reliable."

Since the rod has been put into shape for this summer's trip I have been made happy—No! it's not a new baby, but the next thing to it—a split bamboo. I have it in my mind that an old fellow capable of being made the recipient of a split bamboo, a genuine split bamboo (the donor for my guaranty), with the name of the maker upon it as a warrant to all the world, will be elevated in your estimation. I am that he. With this poem in my hand I yet felt as of the stone age. I have not been educated up to this standard. I don't know what to do with it. I never felt just exactly the same way but once before, and that was a little short of a year after I was married, and I thought I had got used to that sensation, but when my generous friend put into my hands this miracle of grace and artistic skill, the old feeling came back, and I was "two inches taller." That, I believe, is the orthodox expression for such occasions.

It is said that hope ends in fruition; except in the matter of babies and split bamboos, I believe this to be true.

If you are bored with this effusion, lay it to my split bamboo, upon that hint I spake; for the rod, you know, is an emblem of affliction, save in your own hand.

Troublesome

ONY Weller tells us of a friend he had, who, becoming misanthrope, went for revenge and kept a "pike," in this country commonly called a tollgate. The frequency of tollroads and the rates of toll in Colorado would make the state a paradise for misanthropes. One gate may be located every ten miles, so the law provides, and you are sure to find them if you travel ten miles on any road. Some fellow has said that all roads lead to Rome, but in this country all roads lead to turnpikes. It was a delightful conceit of old Tony's, but if I wanted to reach the seventh heaven of revenge I'd hunt out a location on any road five miles from a tollgate and open a house of entertainment for man and beast. The entertainment for the beast would be a mere poetic license, a sort of wild fancy, and consist of illimitable acres of rocks and pine brush;

a picket pin and a lariat, if the beast was to grow gaunt. Leave out the picket pin and the beast would entertain himself by running away; but it would be my custom, nevertheless, to charge fifty cents per head "all the same," and get it, because no one in this country ever thinks of disputing the landlord's demands. I'd say to you, "Thar was the pastur; you turned your hoss in thar; ef he's strayed, that's your lookout, not mine; I'll claim a lien on the one that's left, for the feed of both." The law allows it and the court awards it. No use to suggest that the horse may not have been in the "pastur" half an hour; "the pastur was thar, prepared for the hoss, and ef the hoss strayed, that's your lookout, not mine." If you were reasonable I would give the remaining horse the run of the "pastur" and charge you for it while you hunted up the stray. If you'd "kick" there might be trouble, and trouble under the circumstances in this country might be serious. But the cream of the business of wayside entertainment would be in the cooking, and the results of it thrown together for the man. I'd fry everything; would rack my ingenuity for a method of frying the chicory. Two dishes for flitch and potatoes, rolling-prairie-dried-apple-pie and griddle cakes would be a red-letter day in the calendar of any tenderfoot who chanced my way. If a man hinted at a teaspoon to eat his blasted blackberries, I'd wither him with a glance of my frontier eye, and ask him if he thought I kept a Denver restaurant. Tony Weller's friend no doubt did the best "according to his lights," and opportunities, but the capabilities of my plan, with study, are boundless. Imagination runs riot on the theme, and the only wonder to me is that some fellow, misanthropically inclined, has never adopted this method of making his fellows happy. Perhaps there are no misanthropes in Colorado. At least I am away from them, tollroads and wayside houses; in the land of the mosquito and the trout; and the meadowlarks perch upon my tent top and "give salutation to the morn," by conjugating the to them familiar Greek verb—at least it strikes me so.

Mosquitoes are among the blessings of this life; they prepare us for the robes of immortality, by teaching us patience under affliction. If there is anything I love better than a mule, it is a mosquito. There is poetry in his flight and music in his song. Never having concealed my love, I think it got abroad and preceded me this trip. I found him and his family here, on the banks of the Troublesome; there is quite a number of him, so to speak, and he keeps one's five senses actively employed at once, while he inculcates prudence and fortitude. I met a man from the mouth of Troublesome, and he told me he had seen but one mosquito, and "he was very wild." That is the one I have been looking for; I long to cultivate him, on the same principle that a fellow wants the girl, not the whole family. The Mississippi gallinipper is adolescent compared to the Troublesome mosquito. Yesterday I saw one stick his bill into a gallon jar and take a drink without any apparent effort. If I had anticipated the pleasure, I would have borrowed some foils and got up a few fencing matches. I wouldn't under any consideration suggest broadswords or cavalry sabres, for that might prove dangerous. I am maturing a plan to submit to the Secretary of War, whereby I think the mosquitoes of this immediate vicinity may be advantageously organized in a campaign against the Utes. Judiciously maneuvered, they'd exterminate the Indian. West Point can boast of no such natural drillmasters. Their individual proficiency in this regard makes me itch to present my project to the department at Washington. All they need for effective service is regimental discipline, and I have no doubt our representatives in Congress can find some of their unemployed military constituents at the Capital who would prove excellent and willing disciplinarians. Salary, of course, would be of no consequence; love of country, something to do except turning up their toes in her service, would be ample pay. The more I reflect upon this project of mine, the better I think of its possibilities, and, but that this world is given to ingratitude, the debt that Belford and our two Senators would owe me for thus opening one channel for their relief would be great. I believe "there's millions in it."

But how about the trout fishing? you ask.

Well, the trout fishing is good. I have met the usual tourist, with cod hooks, chalk lines and wagon poles, with an occasional hatful of highly colored flies; the fellow with the hundred dollar rig and helmet hat, apparently all "fly," and I have seen them belabor the beautiful Grand for a mile at a stretch, my mind dwelling on murder. The "swish" of their poles through the air sounds like the slough of an amateur cyclone, and the fall of the lines upon the water as though some indignant father were having an interview in the woodshed with his firstborn, and nothing handy but a quarter strap. Could the fishing be otherwise than good? Good for the fishermen because it gives them plenty of exercise, and as half at least of the pleasure of this life is made up of anticipation, these fellows keep thinking all the time that they are going to catch something, and they do—cold. Good for the trout because they are never caught, and good for the sportsman who knows their ways, though they be like the "way of the serpent upon the rock"—past finding out. The instinct of the trout is akin to the sense of the human sucker, and I have sometimes wondered if they did not entertain a pretty fair idea of our lunatic asylums, and gain the impression that at certain seasons there was an exodus; that the inmates escaped into the wilderness and deployed along the mountain streams; that these people were the descendants of farmers and laborers opposed to the probable innovations of threshing machines, and esteeming the ancient flail above all other methods, thus expressed their hallucination. It requires no stretch of the imagination to thus consider.

There is no genuine enjoyment in the easy achievement of any purpose; there is no bread so sweet as the hard-earned loaf of the man who works for it. The rule holds good in the school of the sportsman. The fellows I have been writing of, had they their way, would become mere engines of destruction; they would catch, not for the pleasure of catching, but because they could, and a universe of trout would not satiate them. Sportsmen are not made of that kind of material. A little horse sense goes a great way in all things, trouting not excepted; it is an indispensable foundation to success. Avarice must be ruled out; your genuine angler has none of it, but will insist on his neighbor having at least as good as he, if not better.

I said awhile ago that I was away from toll-roads and wayside houses of entertainment. I'm stopping with a friend, a genuine angler, whom I have seen walk in the wake of one of those threshing machines, with a rod light as a buggy whip, and with a twist of the wrist drop a fly upon the water thirty or fifty feet away, and as it settled gently down, as falls the snowflake upon the bosom of the stream, there would come a rush and struggle that denoted the fishing was really good to him who had achieved the art of casting a fly.

He is no seeker after distinction, and I shall not give you his name. He does not read Horace, nor does he understand the thirty-nine articles of the established church, as some of our amateur Christians do, but he knows how to treat his friends, which is better. I had been tickling my vanity with the belief that I knew something about trout fishing, but I have found out that my acquirements were, by way of comparison, merely with the escaped lunatics. He sends me out to "take the cream off" a pool, or out of it, and when I'd be ready to swear there was not another left, he'll make me bear witness to my own lack of faith by striking as many, if not more, than I had brought to creel. He thinks I'll learn to handle a fly rod after awhile, and I have hope; besides I am learning to cultivate all the virtues. Think of me with the mercury at seventy or more at high noon, rubber boots with tops to my hips, thick breeches, woolen shirts and a duck coat, my intellectual head swathed in a net and my horny hands encased in buckskin gauntlets, a ten-ounce fly rod, and ten pounds of trout brought to basket at my back, perspiration exuding in streams; outside that net nine thousand mosquitoes to the square inch, yet I'm happy—going to school, and have the best of the vermin.

Meteorological

Hot weather is pleasant to have—in Denver—and I didn't escape because of hot weather. But I have lived there a long time and know a number of people, and every time I met a fellow on the street he was sure to say: "Hot, ain't it?" Five minutes after, if I met the same man, he would pull off his hat, mop his head with a handkerchief, and as if it had just occurred to him, tell me the same thing, with an emphatic prefix. By way of change it is interesting to see a couple of fellows meet on the sidewalk, shake hands, and hear them tell each other "it's hot." The amount of information mutually imparted is gratifying, and makes one think, at first, that life is worth living. But when this delight is experienced a hundred times a day for a couple of weeks, one begins to sigh for the old standby: "What's new?" "Nothing." The monotony becomes exasperating, and even one not given to profanity stands in imminent peril of falling into the prevailing habit. Shakespeare, Mother Goose, or some other mortal plethoric with wisdom, has informed us that evil associations corrupt good manners. I was being led astray; I knew it, in fact.

The air was becoming thickly freighted with expletives; heat and profanity, as I had been taught to believe, before "the new version," were inseparable. The maternal admonition came back to me in all its bitter sweetness, and I had the fortitude to shun the temptation. In the classic language of this age, "I lit out" for lighter air and a purer atmosphere; I did not find what I wanted until I got beyond Golden. When the train entered the canyon the sublime grandeur of—but I promised not to say anything about Clear Creek Canyon, as that has been written about once before. I took it all in, however, cinders included; all except "that mule." I have never been able to find "that mule." Several years since I was advised of the existence of "the mule," and though I firmly believed at the time that my informant was only trying to make himself agreeable, I have, upon every occasion, faithfully looked out from the mouth of the canyon to Beaver Brook for the picture of that much-abused hybrid. The nearest approach to success in my efforts was a spotted cow, three years ago, browsing among the rocks—but she is not there now.

At Dumont a friend of mine climbed on the

train, and the first thing he said to me was: "It's hot in Denver." He did not speak interrogatively, but the remark was affirmative, in a tone of defiance. I asked him if he had ever heard of Billy the Kid. He said he had and that he was dead. I told him that was a mistake, "He is not dead," said I, "he's on the train with me. I have hired him to go as far as Empire to kill the first man who says the word 'hot' to me. There he sits," and I pointed to our very sedate fellow-townsman, Judge—, who sat behind us deeply immersed in a formidable bundle of law papers.

"The devil!" said my friend.

"Yes, he is, and a dead shot; let me introduce you—come."

"Excuse me, my wife is in the other car, just up from Denver, and I havn't seen her for a week. Some other time I'll be happy."

I do not understand why it is that this generation is so given to lying. That friend of mine is not married, and he must know that I am aware of it; yet he slid out of the car with all the bustle of a conscientious man of family. In fact he was too anxious, except for a Benedict in the honeymoon. When he left I went over and sat down by the Judge. In the meantime the latter had folded up his papers and wanted to know of me, first thing, if I had ever read Pompelli or some other fellow, who had traveled in Abyssinia, where the mercury stood habitually at 150°, when you could find a shady place for the thermometer; where the natives cut steaks out of the live oxen, sewed up the wounds and cooked the meat in the sun; where these same natives went about naked with rawhide umbrellas, and each fellow carried a pair of tweezers in his pocket to pull the cactus thorns out of his feet. While being entertained with these veracious statements, I discovered that our car had suddenly become quite full, and that the Judge and I were objects of interest. Just then the engineer sounded the whistle for Empire, and I gathered up my creel and gripsack of commissaries, and made for the door. As I got off the platform I heard one passenger tell another that "the reward is $2,000," and as the train started on I noticed the Judge in animated conversation with a burly fellow whose prominent features were a heavy moustache and a square jaw. The Judge is a good man—physically, I mean—but I shall not see him again for a month, and if it comes to the worst, roughing it in the hills has a tendency to take off flesh and put on muscle. I take comfort in the reflection.

At Empire I found my conveyance awaiting me—a light wagon and a pair of playful mules; little fellows with coats of satin and gentle eyes. Some fellow would say they had "sinews of steel," but these mules were not built that way; they were the natural sort. I dearly love a mule, and were I a poet, would write a sonnet to a mule's eye. I admire a mule's eye; always feel interested in that portion of his anatomy, and, as one likes to be in the vicinity of that which is pleasing, so I, when I have any business with a mule, find his head the attractive feature. These mules behaved remarkably well; they took us to the top of Berthoud Pass in about three hours, and climbed over each other only twice during the trip. That, however, was only in playfulness; they pretended to be frightened, in one instance at a laborer's coat lying by the roadside, and in the other at an empty fruit can. I thought on both occasions that the mountainside was steeper, the gulch ever so many million feet deeper, and the road narrower than any other place I had ever been in. But as the mules were only in fun, I did not feel scared. After the first exhibition of hilarity the driver told me that the last stranger who rode behind those mules had his neck broken by jumping out of the wagon. I know the driver to be an innocent young man, unversed in the wicked ways of this world, and it was comforting to be in congenial company.

On the summit Captain Gaskill handed me his thermometer. I don't know why he did it; I had not said anything about the temperature. But I saw the mercury rise in the tube the moment I touched it; I told him to take the blasted thing away or I would melt right there; with my heavy overcoat on I would have been a mere spot in ten minutes. He hung the agitator on the side of the house, and it registered 45°. I felt cool, and he took me to the fire. No one that I know of except Hamlet's father has returned to give us any authentic information from beyond the sea; and how it was ascertained that "in the twinkling of an eye" we mortals should realize the end of our journey from this shore, I am not prepared to say. But I can vouch for the fact that it was just eight hours from Denver to happiness. If dissatisfied humanity demands a country better adapted to its wants than Colorado, it will have to die to find it.

Upon a former occasion several years ago, I took upon myself to say publicly through the columns of a Denver daily, that I thought Coates Kinney's "Rain on the Roof" a satire. But the night before I had lain in a pool of water on the banks of the Blue with nothing between me and the angry heavens except my prayers for daylight; they, of course, were thin but earnest. This night, however, I had, as the preacher used to say, "a realizing sense" of the effect of surrounding circumstances, repented me of my harsh verdict, and hope to be forgiven. I had supper, a not uncommon event on the top of the range at this particular point. Thanks to the mules (they had allowed me to walk a mile or more) and the light air, and wholesome food well cooked, and the obliging host and his wife (think of their hibernating, the snow level with the ridgepole, and never a soul to visit them except the mail carrier on snowshoes), I had an appetite, and made good use of it, while the clouds gathered outside for a jubilee. After supper came the indispensable pipe and chat, and then to bed, right under the rafters, with the rain pattering on the shingles.

> It seemed as if the music
>   Of the birds in all the bowers,
> Had been gathered into rain-drops
>   And was coming down in showers.

There is only one line of Kinney's poem that ever troubled me (the foregoing is not his):

> Then in fancy comes my mother.

When I was a boy I didn't fancy my mother coming around my bed after I had crawled into it. It meant something besides prayers for me; we had hard timber in the country where I was born and bred—how pliant the young twigs were! Coates must have been a good boy, especially with such a name; I can solve the mystery in no other way. But all that about "another,"

> With her eyes delicious blue,

will do "passing well," except the color; mine were not blue, and she played the same game on me.

With the "patter of the soft rain overhead," I soon forgot all about the thermometer and the other misfortunes, being wrapped in—forty pounds of blankets.

Having gone to bed, it is a very good place to stop; and as to the trip down to the Springs, if those mules give me any trouble I will let you know about it.

Mules

"THE morn, in russet mantle clad, walks o'er the dew of yon high eastern hill." That was my matutinal orison as I tumbled out of bed at Gaskill's. The air was fragrant with the perfume of the pine, and the hardy wildflowers were brilliant in liquid diadems. Some other fellow would say that he "drank in the life-giving tonic;" but I don't drink, so I breathed it, with my head out of the garret window, and felt as though this world has some things to enjoy, and that fresh air is one of them. The blue seemed nearer, and as I looked over into the Park, and over the fir-crowned hills to the majestic piles of granite, everywhere set off with a background of azure, I felt as though there was a mistake somewhere in my makeup. I ought to have been born with a gift to make the whole world feel as I did then—happy but humiliated among these magnificent monuments of Divine greatness. I'm not a self-made man, that's the trouble; if I'd had the ordering of it, I'd have got up a success. There is nothing like success, even in a fraud, until it stands face to face with such evidences of the sublime handiwork as I looked out upon that bright morning; then the "uses of this life" seem "flat, stale and unprofitable," as we use them.

But I must not forget the mules. Gaskill has a couple of cinnamon bears, in a room at the end of the barn. I can't say that the Devil got into the mules, because the Devil is now ruled out; without a hell to put him in, he is no longer of any earthly use. I am sorry to lose him, because under certain circumstances I am a believer in intimidation; it is wholesome. I have known a single quiet and orderly hanging in a summary way, to make a neighborhood that would have terrorized Satan himself, as nice and well behaved as a community of Quakers. I heard one of our Denver preachers once say—and we all loved him—that there was "a certain class of mortals whom it was necessary to take by the neck and choke before they could be made ready for conviction." The Devil has always been useful for that purpose, and I think he could be made available yet.

But I started to say something concerning those mules. The Devil, as I have said, did not get into the mules, but they got scent of those bears, and I venture the assertion that the bears discounted the Devil in his palmiest efforts, as heretofore reported.

To speak without exaggeration, those mules were frightened; the bears were in their heads, heels, hair and eyes; inside and out, above and below, and all around, were bears. To those mules, it rained bears, and the atmosphere was pregnant with bears about to be delivered. If those mules had been human I would have thought it the worst case of delirium tremens that ever racked a diseased imagination. As the driver expressed it: "they was plumb crazy." There was no crookedness about it; they were frightened horizontally as well as straight up and down, as I suppose the driver meant to be understood. It is impossible for me to tell what they did or attempted. They seemed capable of any extravagance except dying. I like to ride after mules in that condition; there is something exhilarating in dashing down a mountain road with one's hair straightening out behind as though it would disappear by the roots; careening around short curves and making lightning-like estimates of the thousands of feet to the bottom of the gulch; picking out the softest rocks upon which to fall; flying over boulders and becoming entangled in tree tops fifty feet in the air, there to remain a torn and wretched monument of indiscretion. It wouldn't be much of a monument, but enough to tell the tale. I thought how grand it would be, and told the driver that I preferred to have him pick me up whole some distance down the road; I felt confidence in my ability to control my own legs; the air was just right for a brisk morning walk; besides, much of the pleasure of the ride would be denied me by reason of my not having any hair to speak of that might stream in the wind. I made these suggestions and started. I believe the driver thought I was afraid to ride after those mules; but that was a mistake. I intended to ride after them provided there was anything to ride in when he should catch up to me, if he ever did. About two miles down the range I sat on a log and waited for the wreck. Presently I heard the rumbling of the wagon; soon it came in sight, the driver sitting at his post singing, as well as the roughness of the road would permit: "I want to be an angel." I certainly thought he did, and asked him if the mules had not tried, at least, to run away, when they were being harnessed.

"Oh, no; they was too bad scared. You see, when they get that way they want to stay right with me; a mule is an obstinate cuss, you know, and only runs away for fun."

Just then the ears of the off mule stuck out straight as the prongs of a magnified clothes pin, and she began to dance. This time it was a ground squirrel, not much larger than a lead pencil. But the brake had to come down before the mule did. Shortly after, the nigh mule went through a like performance for a similar cause, and then they both waltzed to the music of the Frazier. I was sorry when we got as far as Cozzens', because there it was plain sailing, with plenty of room to turn around and run away in, and yet those delightful mules trotted right along twenty-two miles to the Springs, regardless of gophers, old clothes, tin cans and two badgers. If Gaskill's bears had got in the way, I firmly believe those mules would have trotted over them, or kicked them out of the road. Kick! They could kick in pure cussedness. "*I should say so.*"

A mule is a natural kicker, as a rule, but this pair had so improved upon nature's gift, by constant practice, that they had reduced the accomplishment to an exact science. "They can fetch anything they go for, from a gnat on a stall post to a self-confident hostler." "The nigh mule can take a fly off her right ear with her nigh hind foot." I can't describe how she does it, not having seen the feat performed, but the driver explained it to me so that I understood it. From my confidence in the veracity of the driver, but especially from my knowledge of the mule, I am ready to be sworn. But it is about time these mules were lost.

We have the usual complement of campers and tourists in the Park this season. The former are mostly of our own mossbacks; but it will not do to call the tenderfoot by any less dignified title than a tourist. I saw one of the latter start out the other morning for a day's sport. He had a rifle and a shotgun, a gamebag, a fishing rod and creel; he remarked to me, as he climbed up on the off side of his horse, that he was pretty well fixed for a day's campaign. I told him I thought he was, but suggested that he ought to take along a bass drum to beat up the game, and, do you know, the fellow got mad and made me apologize. If he had only kept me in front of his infernal arsenal, I never would have modified my suggestion, but he threatened me over his shoulder, and that looked dangerous. He came back at night, to my surprise, but brought neither fish, flesh nor fowl; it is perhaps needless to say he was the only disappointed party in the Park.

A strict enforcement of the game and fish law would be an advantage to this vicinity. The Park is easy of access, and when the railroads, or either of them now under construction, shall be completed, the Park and its surroundings, a very paradise for sportsmen, can be made the most attractive resort in the state. Why, it is worth a day's journey to sit where I do now, under the shadow of a pine whose every sigh in the cool breeze is freighted with fragrance, and feast on the massively beautiful scenery. A foreground of a mile or two of meadow rich in green and gold; the beetling lava cliffs on the left, and the brown hills, studded with great piles of granite, sloping gently down to the margins of the Grand. The noble stream flecked with silver, rolling majestically along and keeping time to its own melody, while away beyond lies the range for a background, with Long's Peak, o'ertopped with fleecy clouds to serve him as a diadem, to be changed to a turban of rainbow tints for evening dress. And the sunsets that gather about the head of the rugged giant! You who view them from the other side should sit under the shadow of Mount Bross and see the cloud tints that crown His Majesty. Your view from the eastern side shows but the work of a tyro; from this the accomplished task of the master. If I had the gift I spoke of, you should see it as I do; as it is, there is nothing left but to come over and take it in for yourself. You can have a change of program everyday, and when you tire of the pictures, if you can, it is easy climbing a few hundred feet to find a dozen others just as grand and no twins. I suppose many a fellow has glanced over his shoulder up the Grand and seen a mountain with a notch in it, no more, not even a patch of color. But ten to one of these have seen something more and yet made a hearty meal of flitch and potatoes.

Music and Meteorology

WITHOUT fair success with rod and line, a camping trip, to some at least, would be a failure. The weather giving fair promise, I started over the divide below the Springs to revisit several familiar pools and riffles down the Grand, in anticipation of a good morning's sport. The forenoon was expended with half a dozen trout and as many miles' tramp as the result. Life is not worth living without a disappointment now and then. I met with a decided failure where I had rarely had anything but success, and it sharpened my appetite — for dinner.

A day or two after I was joined by my familiar and guide, the Doctor, who is an animated encyclopedia not only of the Park, but of the state, and we forthwith put up a job, as it were, upon the denizens of Williams' Fork. Nine o'clock found us on the banks of that beautiful stream, our horses picketed and we ready to meet any emergency that might arise—that's a new name for 'em. The Doctor started up stream and I took to the bed of the creek about half a mile from its mouth. Twenty minutes and not the sight of a fin. I also began to think that Williams' Fork was depleted. Brown hackles and gray, and a half dozen other newfangled varieties not named to me, had no more effect than the wiles of a three-card monte dealer have upon one who "has been there." I thought of lying down upon the bank and seriously playing with the garter snakes, but changed my mind and put on a gray hackle with a peacock body. Result, a trout. I had found the color to tickle their fancy for the day.

Trout and—and—women are very much alike; few men know much about either, unless you take their own words for it. Both are handsome, of course, delicate in taste, fickle as to ornament, not otherwise, and always too confiding in that which is least to be relied on. I felt sorry for that trout as I slipped her into my creel; they are such short-sighted fish—I'll not say why—but they exact the angler's care, and carry out the simile admirably. Had I offered that trout a worm for breakfast, the chances are ten to one she would have inquired whether I took her for a sucker. But it occurs to me all at once that I am on delicate ground—the current runs five miles an hour; the water is above my knees and the rocks are slippery; to fall is easy as—lying; the fate of our common ancestor is a warning.

By the time I had reached the Grand I had about seven pounds of fair-sized trout, besides having returned with all possible gentleness to the water a number of small-fry. I did not consider it much of a catch, as upon more than one occasion over the same ground I had filled my fourteen-pound creel in the same time. The Grand looked tempting as I waded out into the deep, clear current at the confluence of the streams, and dropped the peacock as far out in the deep pool as I could. I took that fly out in a hurry as I saw the gaping mouth of a leviathan, to my imagination, about to take it off. I speedily had the fly changed to one upon which I could rely, and commissioned it to that pool on business of moment. It had no sooner touched the surface than the glistening sides of my much-coveted triumph shone in the brilliant sunlight, clear of the water, as he darted for the fly and—missed. I thought the fish a little nervous, and I sent the falsehood over into the pool again; as soon as it touched the tiny wavelets that roofed the haunt of his excellency he was again visible, shooting from out the depths straight to his destiny. He reached it, and for a second lay poised as if in inquiry, and then, realizing that he had "struck it," disappeared as suddenly as he had come. I realized, too, that I had struck it. There was music in the air—the music of the reel—and that trout danced to the measure with fifty feet of line before he allowed an inch of slack. He was nervous; there was plenty of water, a hundred feet at least, to the opposite bank, and miles up or downstream; there was no reason whatever for uneasiness—on the part of the fish I mean. But he seemed as much disturbed as ever when the slack was all in, and I, quietly and in as dignified but determined a manner as smooth stones and rubber boots would permit, backed up to the dry beach. Exhibiting the utmost reluctance to being thus led by the nose, he suddenly took it into his head to come voluntarily, started my way, but as suddenly changed his mind; the reel accommodated his whim and played a waltz; the old fellow, however, soon got giddy and asked for a rest; there could be no bar to so reasonable a request, paradoxical as it may seem; I immediately relieved him of the weight of the loose silk and gave him the privilege of a closer inspection of the gentleman at my end of the line. Had any other man been in my place, I should have concluded that the fellow on the fly was not favorably impressed, as he started with celerity on another trip across the Grand. Being myself a man of benignant appearance, I concluded, of course, that he had become enamored of the sound of the reel and was delighted that I had taken a hand in the revelry. Humanity, however, has not the monopoly on making mistakes, and as the reel was evidently taking a turn—this time at a dead march—I towed the gentleman round and gently drew him out on the clean gravel. He measured just nineteen inches; when I first saw him I thought he was "a yard long," but even with his nineteen inches his capacity for conferring happiness was immeasurable. As I relieved his mouth of the hook, the Doctor, who had come down to me unawares, startled me with the remark, "You seem to take a heap of delight in catching a sucker." There was a maliciousness in his tone that led me at once to inquire what success he had met with; his open creel disclosed three only, that would not weigh half as much as my capture; they were the result of his morning's work. My own dignity will sometimes get the better of my reverence, and I read him a homily on envy.

The next day the Doctor proposed a visit to Grand Lake. I suggested that it threatened rain, and he replied that he who went fishing must expect to get wet. The retort, I told him, was dry with age; but the mules were hitched—they have not been lost—and we started up the Grand Valley in the sunshine, but had not been long on the road before it began to rain. Rain is a good thing in the mountains; it freshens up the earth, brightens the wildflowers, fills the air with a new fragrance, makes the grass grow, and I like it. I told the Doctor how much I enjoyed it coming down in vast sheets, but he did not say anything, only smiled. I've seen that smile before; in a fighting man it is dangerous. I didn't say anything more about the rain, but tried to impress him with my knowledge of locations for dairy farms, and the excellence of the neighborhood for the growth of turnips and potatoes for winter food, without irrigation. Toward noon we came to a stream, and he told me it was North Fork; it rained at North Fork. I asked him where the other prongs were. He said there was but one other, "up yonder." I told him the style of fork was long out of date. He stopped the mules. I noticed that smile again, and immediately changed the subject by asking him how far it was to the lake. He said it was about a mile in a direct line, but we did not go that route. About an hour afterwards I asked again how far it was, and he said it was half a mile in a direct line. I was about to inquire why he didn't take the "direct line," but changed my mind, and reflected upon the uncertainty of distances in this light air, and the gratifying exactness of the information one derives from being told something is "up yonder." It rained. Sometime during the afternoon we came to what appeared to me a long line of embankment of gravel and boulders that might have been thrown up by the Titans for a railroad bed in the long ago. We had passed a number of railroad grade stakes, and I inquired if the embankment was the road-bed of the Denver, Utah and Pacific. He said it was a moraine. I thought he was joking, but he always laughs when he gets off a good thing, and he looked as sober as a hired mute at a pauper funeral. I meekly suggested that we had already had more rain than—. He stopped me and the mules right there; said the lake was just over that bank, and had no bottom; that I deserved to be drowned, and wanted to know my weight. I told him that under ordinary circumstances not very heavy, too light to sink, at least, but when wet I swelled. He concluded to go on. It rained, and after awhile we reached the town of Grand Lake. It is hid from the lake, and I was thankful; for I could climb over the moraine—what a handy word for such weather—and look out upon a beautiful sheet of water nearly three miles long by half that in width, guarded at the east and south by mighty hills, while to the southwest I could have recognized Powell Mountain, the grand, with lower hills for distant foreground, and forget the two saloons, the saw mill, tavern and a few slab shanties that were hidden from view—by the moraine—while the clouds hid everything else; and it rained.

We crossed the north inlet and pitched our tent, at the recommendation of a friend, in the midst of a grove of young pines, where the ground was soft with the dead needles from the protecting branches. The couch was delightfully tempting, on the very margin of the lake, with the gentle murmur of the miniature breakers to lull us to sleep.

But it rained; I think, however, I have mentioned that fact; there was another drawback, or rather a number of them—ticks. The next morning another friend exhibited to our wondering gaze about two quarts of fish, something less than a hundred to the quart, and said he caught 'em with grasshoppers. I asked him if the grasshoppers were small. He said they were ordinary grasshoppers. Then I asked him if he had to rip any of them open, and he wanted to know for what, and I said to take the fish out of them, of course. He was a polite friend, and he laughed, but I know him for a mimic. He said the fishing was splendid, and I did not tell him of my nineteen-inch prize, lest he might for the first time doubt my veracity.

After breakfast, it looked as though we might have some "falling weather," and, while I am partial to a little rain after a very long dry spell, I suggested to the Doctor that, considering we had to do some fording, we had better get to the Springs while we might. He went right off and hitched up those mules; never said a word; didn't even ask me to help him. He wanted me to carry away a pleasant remembrance of the lake, so he drove round to the south side. Then it began to rain. It is raining yet, and, to all appearances, is settled weather.

I have been sitting under my canvas roof this blessed day, looking at the rain and watching the meanderings of the tiny rivulets outside, and the midges that congregate about their margins. They stand on the current and ride off, and I sometimes think they come back again to "keep the mill going," as you and I did on the ice when we were younger boys than now. The ground squirrels and chipmunks come out of their holes to pay me brief visits and then scud back. The little chips are cunning chaps, their motions are agile, their eyes are bright, and the glistening raindrops that soak all else, leave no impression upon their glossy fur. They run up the stalks of the wild rye, nibble off a head and drop to the ground as quickly as falls the severed top, and then to shelter under the lee of a log or a projecting rock, to feast. One other visitor I have had today—a solitary blackbird with feathers awry and tail bedraggled. He had a melancholy look in his white eyes as he cocked his head despondingly, and his forlorn condition made me think he might be, in miniature, the larcenous and unfortunate jackdaw of Rheims, suffering under the Cardinal's curse. His wretched condition was contagious, and I myself was about to request him to "move on," when one of his brethren, dressed in blue and sable, a policeman, evidently, in their community, ran him in, or off. For aught I know he may be now before His Honor on the general charge of vagrancy, with a prospect of a fine and costs, or in default of means, with a term in the blackbird jail staring him in the face.

I want to go home. The Grand is brown, Williams' Fork is gold color; the Troublesome is so thick that you can stick a knife into it, turn it round and see the hole. Trout fishing this side Egeria Park is not to be thought of, for it seems to have been raining as it never rained before. As if 'twould keep on raining, evermore.

Philosophy

UPON the contingency of a rainy day it is always pleasant to have something to read in the mountains. A friend of mine gave me a pamphlet written by one Herbert Spencer, entitled "Education." A level-headed appreciative friend who understands one's needs, is a good thing to have. Education was my necessity. After being educated I became hungry for more. My friend had said there were "some good things in Herbert; that he was a philosopher, but given to infidelity." I discovered that Herbert had written a library; I had, then, so to speak, the wide world from which to choose. I am a seeker after happiness, so I selected "Social Statics, or the Conditions Essential to Human Happiness." If there is any one thing that I enjoy more than another, it is happiness. Having secured the key to the "Essential Conditions," I felt as I imagine a hungry and ragged prospector feels when the assayer tells him he has "struck it," and drew heavy drafts on the future, just as any prospector does. The "Essential Conditions," being philosophy, is not dry reading as you may imagine, that is on a rainy day in camp. It is good as a comedy.

Dickens tells us that the editor of the Etanswille *Gazette* employed a savant to write an article on Chinese Metaphysics, and that the learned gentleman did it after this fashion: He consulted the Encyclopedia Britannica, first under the title "Chinese," and second under the title "Metaphysics," and combined his information. The editor gravely informed Mr. Pickwick that the essay caused a sensation, as no doubt it did, and Her Majesty's minions were put on the lookout for an escaped lunatic. Sometimes, while studying the "Conditions"—you study and do not read philosophy—I thought Herbert, when he labored on the "Conditions," must have been a very old man, in his second childhood, for instance, and troubled with dyspepsia. Sometimes that he must have been young, very young, staggering under a heterogeneous load of information that had got the better of his mental calibre; that his mind, so to speak, was in the condition of a few acres of undergrowth just after a hurricane—demoralized, as it were. Sometimes—when his arguments reminded me of a horde of inebriated aborigines, each ready to kill his neighbor—that he must have been in good condition, with a view to sensation and ducats, and that if his theories, conceding he had any, could, by any conceivable method be put into practice, it would be when "chaos was come again," but that his Christian readers wouldn't see the joke, would take him to be serious, and advertise him with abuse.

"There are some good things in Herbert," of course; I enjoyed them; unless a thing is good you cannot enjoy it; the only one to doubt this would be Herbert. He himself is an argument against total depravity, yet if you can find that he admits the contrary as to all humanity, except Herbert, call me Ananias, and his wife too.

What has Herbert Spencer got to do with Middle Park and trout fishing? you inquire. Not anything, except that he says no fellow has a right to own a mine; that if he—the fellow, I mean—finds a good mine, it belongs to everybody, and he must ask everybody's permission to work it and convert the proceeds to his own use. I wish I were everybody, or "Society," as Herbert calls it, I'd go right over to Leadville or Rabbit Ear Range and assert my rights. Being everybody, nobody else would be around to say anything, except the fellow who had the mine. If he undertook to draw his gun, I'd stand up in front of him and argue the point, while I went round behind him and took away his six-shooter. Being everybody, this would be easy to do. Then I'd let the fellow go find another mine, and everybody would go and tell him he was a claim-jumper and "must light out;" and I'd keep on until I had corraled all the good mines in the state. Then I'd go down to New York and interview Mr. Vanderbilt and other millionaires, and convince them that they entertained a mistaken notion as to the ownership of the many odd millions of government securities and sundry monies and valuables, real and personal, said to be in their names. When I'd got all that, I'd buy—no, I wouldn't—I'd take possession of New York; after that I should be capable of anything—except managing Mr. Conkling.

But I hear you inquire again: What has all this to do with Middle Park and trout fishing? Not anything. But that I am puzzled to know, under the circumstances, what I am to do with the gentleman last above named. If Herbert were only here he could, perhaps, help me out of my dilemma; he can set up a dilemma and help himself out of it as easy as—falling off a precipice, and there is nothing hard about that till you get to the bottom. It must be because his dilemmas are all imaginary, or that mine is not a dilemma. Let us see what he says of one of his: "Of this (dilemma) nothing can be said, save that it seems in part due to the impossibility of making the perfect law recognize an imperfect state, and in part to that defect in our powers of expression. As matters stand, however, we must deal with it as best we may." See how he has helped himself out of that! There is a world of wisdom in it all, especially the last sentence, I know, if I could only find it. But that's the trouble with Herbert—You ask him for bread and he gives you a stone. I know I can do as best I may, but I want to know what to do with Conkling; I cannot go on and perfect my monopoly according to Herbert's philosophy without disposing of Roscoe. This planet is not big enough for both. I am in possession of all worth having. It is well demonstrated that two bodies cannot occupy the same space. He is too old to educate. I am, as Herbert's disciple, opposed to coercion. Everybody, that's me, is entitled to his own free will, but here I can't have mine. He says that nothing can be said, and yet all the newspapers of the country, for three or four months, have been saying a great deal. Then he tells me of the difficulty of making the perfect law—that's me, again—recognize the imperfect state—that's Roscoe. But the latter makes me recognize him. What use is there in telling me I may deal with him as best I may? I didn't need a philosopher to tell me that. I want that impossible possibility of Herbert's—a perfect law. I am in some degree mercenary; everybody is. If I had that law it would be a curiosity, valuable as some of the mines voluntarily surrendered, as already stated, and particularly valuable at this crisis. I want to know how to dispose of Conkling.

You ask me again: What has this to do with trout fishing and Middle Park? and what good is it? Nothing, except it is some of Herbert's philosophy considered in a light atmosphere; where the air is thin, and you can see a great way, it is easier discovering obscure objects in the distance. Herbert could not have expressed himself more clearly.

Well, all right; I'll stop right here. But I would like to say just a word about Herbert's style. I like his style—when I can understand what it is. His arguments are something between black-letter Norman-French and a fashionable bonnet. The one is incomprehensible to the ordinary mind, and the other is a delightful combination of vagaries. Goodbye, Herbert. I hope you will have a good time. But if you don't find it harder work traveling over your own turnpike with the load you have on than driving a jack train over a blind trail, you can set me down for a fool or a philosopher—the difference is so slight that one may be happy as either.

The conditions essential to happiness are three, and may be described thus: Two primary, and one primary and secondary, or primary or secondary, depending altogether upon the existence of the two primary. Thus: the first condition essential to happiness is—that is human happiness; "I do not wish to be misunderstood," nor have the happiness of which I am now writing "confounded (nonsense! No, sir) with some other" happiness— an appetite; this is the first primary. (No, sir! I am not a ward politician.) Let me repeat: the first condition essential to happiness is an appetite. The second primary condition essential is a good digestion. Dependent upon these two is the third condition essential, which may be called something to eat. Thus, if the appetite and digestion are good, the third — something to eat — becomes an essential condition and primary. If the appetite and digestion, or either, is impaired, the third essential condition becomes secondary or useless, so to speak. These, the essential conditions, concurring in one man, he is capable of happiness, mental and physical, otherwise not. Observe, I do not affirm he will be or is happy, but that he is capable, merely, of happiness. The conditions essential must concur, however, and in one man. This is a necessity more than a condition, and may be called properly a concurrent necessity, rather than a condition essential. But the appetite requires food. I mean by this that the appetite of the man — and the term is used in a generic sense and includes women — the most superficial thinker will concede without argument that there must be a man to have the appetite; the man, therefore, will be understood thus: The appetite of the man requires food. If he have the appetite and not the food, the conditions are nonconcurrent. If he have the food and not the appetite, there is a similar, but not exactly parallel, nonconcurrence. If he have the appetite and the food and the dyspepsia, which is the corollary of indigestion, and the opposite of good digestion, or equivalent to no digestion at all, there is a lack of the conditions essential. It would seem, therefore, that there are only three conditions essential, but those three must necessarily concur in one man before he can be happy.

I like positive people with positive opinions, not people who are perpetually preferring exceptions. Now I have one of those noncommittal mortals, who is willing to admit that my conclusion is correct, indisputable in fact, *except* that I have not taken into consideration the possible nonconcurrence of the conditions essential in the event that the food, admitted, has not been properly prepared. While I am free to admit that I have not as yet discovered anything aesthetic about the mere operation of eating, and, further, that it is purely an animal necessity, yet I must contend that the preparation of the food is so far secondary as to be a condition non-essential, as I will now proceed to—.

Well, just as you say; I'm never disposed to bore one if I can help it, though you might have so augured in the premises, after reading the title. Do not swear. I give Herbert up with regret; the sun has come out after the rain, and it is delightful outside this canvas house of mine. The air is fresh with the new dampness, and the raindrops will not linger long in the shirt fronts of the mountain daisies. What could I have done this afternoon if not for Herbert?

An Idle Morning at Grand Lake

FROM under the shelter of a friendly pine I look out upon a long stretch of water, two miles and more, to a sloping beach of a few yards in width, and then a belt of young trees growing back to a rugged mountain gorge. The bright green of the new growth contrasts with the time-stained hues of the great piles of rock, and these grow more wild as the eye follows up the defile. Then a white patch, the length of a man's arm and the breadth of a hand, glistens in the rays of the morning sun, here inaudible, but there a roaring waterfall a hundred feet high.

The gorge widens and drifts away to the right and left, but reaching high, with irregular outlines traced against the blue sky; the tints of brown and gray and green intermingle in bountiful confusion, but never wearisome; then, seemingly, blocking up the gorge in huge and awe-inspiring massiveness, a dome-shaped mountain, with miles of base and height far reaching above the growth of vegetation; just below its summit a bed of snow, shaped like a dove, defying the hot rays of an August sun, sparkles like a jewel on the mountain's brow. Silent and grand, it o'ertops the beautiful lake, mirrors its rugged outlines upon the calm surface, and faintly tints the clear waters with the colors of its robes. To the right and left the nearer and lower-lying pine-covered hills reach round and down to the water's edge.

And the lake, a gem in the mountain fastness, how calm it is! There is no melody in the pines this morning, their sighing is hushed, and the lake is still, its smooth surface only dotted here and there with the widening rings made by leaping trout. How deep it is no man knows; how cruel it has been is the subject of many a story within the experience of the whites about its shores, and legends not a few among the red men. Seductive it is in its silent beauty, and treacherous as grand. Cold and relentless as fate, "it never surrenders its dead." The Ute cannot be induced to approach it, and mentions its name with a shudder, while ye gentle angler commits his frail bark to its bosom with commendable prudence. There is no telling when a storm may come; the clouds are not always the harbingers of a gale; it may come when the sky is clearest, and the awkward skiffs that prevail hereabout are not the safest, even under skillful hands.

But as the sun puts behind him the early morning hours, the dark tints of the smooth waters change, and a mile or more away a ray of silver flashes across the lake; its outer line moves my way, and as the tiny waves reach my shore, the breeze that moved them brings the sound of the waterfall. I listen to the melody it sings, always mellowed in its highest notes by the distance, and then dying gradually away as if sighing the requiem of the lost lying buried here, or as fade the last moments of a weird dream.

And, while I am dreaming, a friend of mine, to whom this ripple is a never-failing sign, pulls out into the lake. I mark the long, steady stroke, and wonder how it is that one so long out of practice can feather his oars so well, when he catches sight of me, idling away the time, and stops. But I wave him on, and watch him as he makes for a point on the western shore that we both know; where the light tint of the water changes suddenly to a hue almost black; where the depth on one side the boat is six feet and on the other may be six hundred; where the trout are large, and where we have had many a good fight. In a few minutes he has business on his hands. I can see his rod, against the dark background of the adjacent pines, bend and spring back, and bend again, and then the flash of silvery spray as the stricken trout breaks the surface in his vain effort to free his mouth from the cruel barb. But a few moments, and the mastery is awarded to human skill, and I see my friend hold up his capture for my delectation. In his enthusiasm he does not stop to consider that I have to take a great deal for granted, that I can at best see only a minute something glisten in his grasp; but he takes off his hat, waives it over his head, and I conclude he has a pounder at least. It turned out to be a little short of double that.

As I lazily wave a response of appreciation my boot-heel comes in contact with a small stone. Something in its shape leads me to pick it up; I find it scarred, and know enough to understand that it is a scratched stone from the till. And so my eyes wander from this product of nature's great lapidary over to the waterfall and the mountain gorge, which had been his workshop, how many thousand years ago, who can tell? The beautiful waterfall is all that remains of him, but his handiwork is abundant.

Stretching along the east shore lies a great lateral moraine, even now twenty, and, in places, thirty feet high, made of great rocks, thousands of tons in weight, down to mere grains of sand. How many generations of pines have found precarious foothold there and died, may be conjectured only. But a new growth is springing up, as if it were the pleasure of the present to keep green the grand monument of the dead glacier.

On the narrow beach, with its background of new growth, smolder the dying embers of a campfire. My eyes follow the thin column of blue smoke that rises and wreathes itself among the treetops, and floats away to where desecration has stepped in. The suggestion of primitive life is dispelled by the ridgepole of a mean house obtruding itself above a depression in the moraine, and I know that this is but the best of a number of slab shanties. They are hidden from my sight, but I recognize them as one does a boil.

The first step into the wilderness of life is filled with bright anticipations, and lack of restraint makes one's happiness as limitless as the great unknown into which one is traveling; the second step is monotonous, and one sighs for the promises of the end. The campfire, emblematical of the first step, is passing away; the slab shanty, the sordid, hard existence that makes life a burden, is the second step, and one longs for the third, that may, if nature must feel the weight of our sacrilegious hands, give us the ashler, graceful roofs, broad porches, and the comforts of a new life. Pioneers are lauded for "subduing the wilderness," but deliver me from witnessing the progress of subjugation. I want to be the first, or, that being impossible, the next best thing to do is to wait till the ruin is complete. One can then imagine what the surroundings were; but in the middle period no room is left for imagination—one can neither wonder what it was or will be, and the only thing left is to "unpack my heart with words, and fall a cursing like a very drab."

While my mental anathemas and I are holding high carnival, I am conscious of the presence of something besides the figures of my imagination. Looking around, I discover a dark-complexioned woman, with hair black as night, when cats most do congregate; eyes like jet, square face, all one color—parchment; a mouth that shuts like a steel-trap. Her hair brushed smoothly back, and gathered behind in a great coil, is beautiful; that is all the beauty I see, except, perhaps, a dainty buttoned boot with a high instep. In one hand she holds the end of a small chain, at the other end of which is— yes, a monkey! This predecessor of the missing link looked at me in a sort of dreamily sympathetic way, and I at him. Our commiseration was mutual, and I felt inclined to shake hands with him. His owner was a French woman, of course; I do not think a woman of any other nation, except as a matter of business, would go wandering round among the Rocky Mountains with a monkey. If she had had a hand organ strapped to her back, I could have forgiven her, even if grinding out "Days of Absence." About the time I had "doffed my old felt," we were joined by the other member of the family; he looked like an Egyptian three thousand or more years old. Not understanding French, I stepped into my boat and joined my friend.

I have been making an effort to secure for you a picture of the lake, and though the photographer has been about here frequently, my success has been indifferent. Every view worth having is sure to have a foreground of one or more of the lords of creation, "bearded like the pard," with an arsenal strapped around their bodies, and an expression beaming out from under their broad-brimmed hats that would drive an ordinary man clear into the ground in sheer humiliation. Think of these addle-pated asses posing for exhibition amid scenes that should awaken naught but wonder and admiration, blended with that reverence one must feel in the presence of the Father's works, and have charity if you can. The very boulders against which they lean are satires that will endure the tread of the centuries long after this world shall have forgotten that such fellows or their seed had ever encumbered the earth.

Camping with Ladies and — the Baby

BEFORE the little narrow gauge engines of the Denver, South Park and Pacific with their trains of baby cars went thundering up through the canyons, reaching out for Leadville, the trouting in the Platte was prime. Following the sinuous track, first on one side of the river, then on the other, you can look out to the right and see your engine going west while your car is going east, then your engine starts east or north and you go south or west. Now you crane your neck to catch the top of some overhanging cliffs a thousand feet high, and are suddenly jerked around a curve into a little glade of a dozen acres with a little brook running through it; then you are as quickly yanked into another canyon. If one were drunk no doubt the road would be straight. But thirty-five or forty miles from Denver the canyon grows familiar. Buffalo Creek comes tumbling out from the south, and presently the brakeman puts his head in at the door and shouts: "Pine Grove!" This is the Pine Grove known to travelers who go by rail, but the Pine Grove of twenty odd years ago was six miles away from the river, and the railroad Pine Grove was Brown and Stuart's ranch, the owners of which drove a thrifty traffic in hay.

In August, 1868, I made acquaintance first with the pools and riffles in the vicinity of the old Brown and Stuart's ranch. I clambered up and down the canyon for five or six miles east and west. The rush and the roar of the crystal waters made glorious music, and an hour's fishing would send me laden back to camp. But for all the grand surroundings, the fresh air, the wildflowers and the trout, there was weariness of heart for her and me who made our camp on the margin of the then beautiful stream. There had a little while before crept over our threshold a shadow we all dread, and which had gone out again leaving a wound that would not heal.

But later on, when the cloud with the silver lining had turned a little of its brighter side our way, there came out to us one of your down-east girls, to whom the Great American Desert was a revelation, and these grand old mountains an epic. It was the season for camping, and she was stricken with the mania at once. She approached the subject tenderfootedly, but being assured that nothing was easier, nothing better for city folks, ecstasy was the consequence. Then there suddenly arose an insurmountable barrier.

"What will you do with the Governor?"

"Take him along, of course."

"What! baby sleep in a tent? Be eaten by mosquitoes, rained on and bitten by snakes?"

The prospect was appalling; but then I assured her that fresh air never hurt babies; that mosquitoes were unknown, in August, at least; that rain was such a rarity that I was compelled to go to the creek for moisture, and as for snakes, the rattlers, at least, they never got beyond the foothills; the little gart—ahem—striped snakes were pleasant to have around, and were cleaner than flies. Besides, it was confidently anticipated that baby was about to distinguish himself, and there was no panacea so efficacious for teething babies as the mountain air. That settled it.

The first thing to be looked after was the mess kit—known among the cowboys as the "chuck box." Mine would fit neatly into the tail end of a wagon; was about two feet and a half from top to bottom, and about twelve inches deep; had racks for cups, saucers, plates, knives and forks, and plenty of room for two weeks' supplies of flour and other necessaries. When we wanted to lunch it was an easy matter to drop the tailgate of the wagon, let down the side of the mess kit, and we had a good table; the whole thing was as handy as a pocket in a shirt, and its capacity marvelous. An ordinary lumber wagon with spring seats, an A tent, 7 x 7, for the womenfolk, plenty of rubber ponchos, a change of clothing, wool, of course, all round. All together making an abundance for comfort, and a light load with which the horses could trot along and not half try.

About the hour that Hamlet's father was wont to render himself up to "sulphurous and tormenting flames," we were astir, and before the sun was up we were away. Fifteen miles to the foothills and Turkey Creek Canyon. Towards noon the sun beats down hotly on the plains, and I always make it a point to get to the canyon by ten o'clock at the outside. And this morning we passed Harriman's before ten, and from our shelf on the mountainside we could look out east till plains and sky came together.

Down below us, on the left, six or eight hundred feet, the little creek looked about as wide as one's finger. The road is fairly wide enough for the wagon, with here and there a "turn out," to accommodate passing teams. To the right a perpendicular wall running up a hundred feet; to the left — well, our visitor said she was tired of riding and would like to walk a little; the road was smooth as a floor, and the grade easy. I suggested that horses rarely cut up capers in such places, but the effect of a wrecked wagon and the remains of a mule lodged against a granite boulder half way down the mountain was not to be overcome by any assurance of mine; and walk she did; so did the baby's mother and maid, taking turns in carrying his majesty for a couple of miles. Not having any hills to climb the inconvenience is not so great; but, take a twenty-five pound youngster in your arms, at an elevation of, say nine thousand feet, and undertake to walk up hill; a half mile seems twenty, and at the end of three-quarters you want to lie down, wondering if your lungs are larger than the universe. But like everything else in this life, it becomes easy when you get used to it.

Our first objective point on this trip was Reed's Mill, about thirty miles from home. No trout, but wild raspberries, now in their prime. Did you ever eat any? If not, the first one you put on your tongue will make you "wish your throat a mile long and every inch a palate," with accessible untold acres of berries. There is about them a tenderness and luscious delicacy, a fragrance and even beauty, that makes a cultivated brother look and taste in comparison like a combination of mucilage and sawdust. The "Shepherd" thought when Tom Moore was penning his Loves of the Angels, that he "fed upon calf foot jeelies, stewed prunes, the dish they ca' curry, and oysters." But I don't believe it. Tom was in America once, and I believe he strayed this way, and was inspired by mountain raspberries, with cream so thick "a spider might crawl on't." I do not believe Tom was so much of an animal as Hogg, by his wit, would make him.

But the fruit season is brief, and three or four days in the berry patch set me yearning for running waters, and the delicate salmon-colored fins. So we broke camp and turned into the road for Pine Grove and the Platte. By five o'clock we were fixed to stay, with plenty of pine knots for the campfire and quaking asp to cook with, our only neighbors a couple of "English cousins," owners of the ranch, from whom we could get cream, and butter and milk, and who helped make our evenings "jolly."

Everything being in trim for the proper conducting of household matters, I received orders to "catch a mess for supper." Right in front of our tent, two rods away, a gravelly bar reached from the bank to the water, and the opposite side, fifty feet about, the river ran deep and rapidly. I had never failed securing a trophy from that swirl, and I sent a gray hackle on its mission as near the opposite willows, and as deftly as my skill would permit. I "struck it rich" the first cast; the fraud had barely touched the water before I saw the jaws of a beautiful trout close upon it, and felt his strength at the same instant. Since last summer's experience I have wished more than once that I had been on that occasion the owner of a split bamboo. As it was, the sport resolved itself into a mere trial of strength between tackle and fish. In three seconds he was ignominiously snaked out on the beach, a three-pound trout, the largest I have ever caught, and enough for supper.

The whole family had "swarmed up" the bank, as Dickens would say, to enjoy my discomfiture, but the contemplated taunts were never given breath. I stood in my tracks and landed three more, and, will heart of man believe it? they complained because the three last were not as large as the first. But my merit was established; when I came home empty-handed, which was hard to do, any explanation of mine was "confirmation, strong as proof of holy writ," that the trout would not rise for anything. So much for reputation! I wonder how many fellows there are in the world who enjoy it who are no more deserving than I?

One morning I started down the stream; it was my birthday, and though nothing had been said about that momentous epoch in my history, I felt it incumbent upon me to achieve something out of the ordinary. I did. I fell off a log, head first, into a hole four feet deep. Cold? well, yes! I thought I had struck a moderate-sized Arctic winter. But there was no one "there to see," and I uttered my benison on the man who invented the sun, as I crawled out to the warmth of our daily servant and friend. My creel was not empty and I saved everything, even my temper. When I got back to camp, she who had taken "the long path with me" suggested that I was wet, that an immediate change of garments was imperative. But, having an exasperating disposition to stubbornness, I insisted that every thread must dry where it was, and it did, without even a sneeze, to punish me for not taking a woman's advice. I had been there before.

It was determined that baby and I should tend camp for half an hour or so that afternoon, while the three natural guardians wandered off to the adjacent hillside for wildflowers wherewith to deck the tea table. This was no new business to us. The young man with a pillow at his back, seated in the middle of a blanket rubbing his face with a teaspoon; I lying prone three feet away with my toes beating an occasional tattoo on the soft sward, my chin in my hands and brierroot between my teeth, watching him. There was a bright light in his eyes, and his cheeks were rosy, soft as velvet, yet firm and cool. What is there like the touch of a baby's cheek pressed against your own! You must turn and kiss it, just as you did its mother's the first time you had a right to. But is there anything more ridiculous in life than to see a baby attempt to put a spoon into his mouth before he has got the knack of it? See him hit himself in the eye with it, pretty much as a drunken man would knock a fly off his nose; smear it down his face, with his mouth wide open and turned up like a young robin's, but it misses the place on the way down; he takes it with both chubby fists, looks at it with dignified surprise, as though for the first time aware of its presence, lets go one hand, whacks the spoon against his ear and drags it across his cheek with the same result. But persistence is characteristic of this baby, a quiet determination that has something appalling about it. If there were any raspberry jam on that spoon his face would look worse than a railroad map of the State of New York. Finally, and as it would seem, after all, more by accident than design, the spoon reaches the right place; he twists it round to the distortion of his rosebud mouth; then he looks at me, sees me laughing; the fun seems to dawn upon him; he takes the spoon out of his mouth, pounds the blanket with it, and smiles back at me, and the smile resolves itself into a well-defined laugh.

The sun has just disappeared behind the range, but there is a mellow ray of golden light that lingers about the baby's head that makes me think—think of the one so like him, and from the base of the hill, with her hands full of wildflowers, the tallest of the three starts toward me, and I remember only the sunshine of the long path.

But I forgot to tell you about my camp stove: it is a piece of sheet iron, eighteen inches square, with a hole in the centre, eight inches in diameter; set upon four stones, it makes a first class stove.

Boys and Burros

FROM my outlook under the shade of the old pine I see a familiar and massive pile of granite over fourteen thousand feet high, and a bit of the range, with patches of last winter's snow glistening in the sunlight. The brown and gray of the lofty peaks are contrasted with the mist-covered blue of the lower mountains. Then comes the farthest glimpse of the beautiful river rolling out from the beautiful canyon of lava cliffs. Then the meadow for a foreground, its rich green tinted here and there with the gold that denotes the coming sickle time. Then the quiet, straggling village of log houses, with its tavern perched upon a hillside, and down by the river bank the smith's shop, where seems the only sign of life. The ring of the "ten-pound-ten," as it comes up to me clear and resonant upon the pure air, does not mar the harmony of the river's melody, nor taint the romance of the scene. But a boy, taking his afternoon nap astride a shingle horse on the shady side of a cabin, does; he is suggestive of some of the realities of life, and is recuperating for my benefit. That shingle horse is to him a bed of roses, and the hard log of the old cabin a pillow of down. He can sleep standing on his head, I believe; I know he can crosswise or tangled up. I am not near enough to see, but I know that his cheeks are red, his face tanned to russet, his hands dirty, his clothes ragged, and—his pulse regular. I know exactly what he will do when he awakes; he'll whistle, whistle for me, but not for my benefit. If he'd only whistle Put Me in My Little Bed, Yankee Doodle, or other soul-moving melody, his music would not be so much a burden. But he cannot distinguish between Gray Eagle and the Doxology; he could whistle a stave from a barrel sooner than a bar from an opera. He whistles to make a noise; and, not content with ordinary methods, he sticks his fingers in his mouth, and awakens the echoes down the canyons until you would think the Utes had escaped from the Reservation and were round hunting scalps.

How did I come by him? Why, through his mother, of course; did you ever know of a boy being round to make life a joy forever, without his mother being at the bottom of it? I had an interest in the boy; his mother is a near relative of mine, and hearing that I was to have a short vacation in the mountains, she thought it a splendid idea, if you know what that is, to have him spend his vacation with me instead of running round the streets. I told her I was going a great way off, into a rough country where the mosquito and buffalo gnat were rampant, to sleep upon the bare ground, to live upon flitch and potatoes with flapjacks fried in grease, and she said that was just what he needed, fresh air and plain food. I told her that where I was going the boys were wicked and the men drank and swore like pirates, and there were no Sabbath schools; she said he would never be good for anything were he not thrown in the way of temptation, and as to the Sabbath school, I could take along a Testament and read to him; that would be novel to myself and amuse the boy. I told of high mountains and dangerous trails to be traversed, of deep caravans and antres vast, of swift rivers, and Utes whose heads were filled with vermin, "the chief end and market of whose time" was to capture and torture boys. She said he would have something to tell about when he came back, and as to the vermin, I could have his head mowed with a clipping machine. I swore I wouldn't take him; but she said she knew I would, and was right, because I always like to, and do, have my own way, except —.

Yes, he is waking up and looking round in search of his Barlow, perhaps. I saw him stabbing the shingle horse with it when he went to sleep.

No, he is not looking for his Barlow, but another fellow of later date. There goes his hand to his mouth; I knew it.

"Hello, old fellow! Here I am under the old pine."

"All right," came back to me, in confidence of my ability to take care of myself, while he had me in sight.

"Can I come up there?" and he granted his own request, as usual.

"What's that thing over there?"

"What thing, and where do you mean?"

"Why, that thing over yonder; it looks like a man."

"I don't see anything that looks like a man."

"Why, don't you see that thing up against that mountain that runs down to the river? It looks like a man with his fist doubled up goin' to hit somebody."

"I see a brown patch against the mountainside surrounded by green that has something the shape of a man—is that what you mean?"

"Yes, what is it?"

"A patch of brown surrounded by grass or bushes."

"Well, what does it mean?"

"I don't know."

"How did it come there?"

"Because the grass or bushes grew around it, I suppose."

"Well, but I mean does it mean anything? It looks like a big man."

"Life is short, little boy. But if it means anything, it is the photograph of the presiding genius of the Hot Sulphur Springs."

"What's a presiding genius?"

"Little boy, did you say that you would like to ride horseback? Yes—well go over and tell the man at the barn that you want the pony."

I am a great lover of ponies; they give one a rest. In fact, if it were not for this particular pony, the only nonbucking bronco in the vicinity, I should be constrained to leave. I have been anxious to go down the river to the house of a friend and have a week's fishing, but I dare not go away from that pony. I am afraid the owner of that pony is mercenary; he refuses to hire him for a week; I think he knows that I want to go fishing, and has possessed himself of the idea that I cannot fish without the pony. He told me only yesterday that he commonly fished off that pony's back; in fact that it was "the best way to fish anyhow." It may be a good method; I never tried it; the novelty of the thing is something of an inducement. But the man asks too much, I am satisfied; the pony is not worth more than thirty dollars, but the owner demands fifty. He says I can sell him again, and I have no doubt of that. But what can I get for him? Well, he don't know, but he's sure I "won't lose nothin'"; he might take a notion to buy him back, at a discount, of course. I offer to pay him the "discount" for the pony's use, and also tender references as to my integrity. But he "don't know nothin' about references—there's the pony, sound in wind and limb, and so gentle a child can ride him, and the best pony to fish off'n I knows on; you can take him, or leave him."

I have concluded to take him; an indifferent saddle and bridle, ten dollars—total, sixty dollars. The boy takes the outfit under his immediate supervision and we go down to the house of my friend.

Here we found another boy a couple of years younger. I did not know of this boy save by report, but now I do. This last boy is sedate; sometimes I think he is about sixty, but his father is not that old, and it bothers me occasionally to determine which is the father and which the son. They call him Judge, and it's worth half a dollar to hear him call me counselor—the title with which he dubbed me on our introduction.

"Counselor, I'm glad to see you; the fishing is good; the mosquitoes are a little troublesome for this time of year; but we can give you a net, and I'll show you where to fish."

His hair is curly, and he has what the mother of the boy in charge of me would call a "sweet face." I was about to take him in my arms, but I took off my hat instead, and introduced him to my boy; they looked at each other, grinned and shook hands; then I knew he was a boy, and again wanted to take him in my arms, but dared not. That evening I sat on a stool mending a broken leader, and the Judge sat opposite in a high chair.

"Counselor," said he, "you are not tying that knot square; that knot will slip; bring it here and let me tie it for you."

I obeyed reverently; he accomplished the trick deftly and handed back my leader in silence.

"Judge, can you tie a fly?"

"Not very well; but I will some day, and then I'll make the trout round here think they are eating candy."

"By the way, Judge, do you like candy?"

"Yes, sir, I do."

I was glad of that, because I'm fond of candy myself, though I never before took any on a camping trip.

We have been at my friend's house nearly a week. I have not as yet had an opportunity to test the qualities of the pony "to fish off'n," but the boys corroborate the stableman's assertion, and I think that unless I can get a good price from the man of whom I purchased him, I shall take him home with me and try him another season. The idea, however, is not of my own suggestion; my boy proposed it. Besides, some day when the boy is at school—blessed be the school, the school teacher, and not the birch—his mother might get a chance to ride. The pony could rest at night, of course. It would only involve a dollar a day and a sidesaddle. Think of a pony eating himself up once a month! That kind of financiering is what keeps me a pauper; I shall have to forego the pleasure of fishing "off'n that pony."

At my friend's house our tent is pitched on the bank of the river. I came away from home to be out. I have slept in the house for so many years that it has ceased to be a novelty. The boy and I sleep together; or rather he sleeps on the same spruce boughs or hay that I occupy. Perhaps there is nothing in the world so beautiful as a sleeping child, with the rosy flush of health mantling brow and cheek, with, maybe, a tear trembling on the closed lashes, the remembrance of a sorrow that was, but now forgotten. This has been an inspiration to a multitude of poets, but the inspiration did not come upon them in camp, nor were the poets trying to snatch repose in the same bed; they were lookers-on merely, giving the rein to their imagination. A poem under such circumstances would be a satire, certainly.

Last night the boy went to bed early, while the pony sorrowfully partook of his evening meal in my friend's meadow. I flattered myself that a good night's rest was in store for me, and turned in as the moon came up over the range. The night was very still, and I was dozing off under the soothing melody of the swift flowing river on its road to the sea, when I thought I heard the distant lowing of a cow; that was no strange matter in this neighborhood. I forgot it in a moment and was gone, perhaps five minutes, trout fishing, or eating wild raspberries with cream, yellow cream, not blue, when I heard the cow again, then something like three hundred cows and as many calves, and six hundred cowboys, all yelling like a band of Apaches just before daybreak. If you never heard an Apache yell, remember, the first time you do, each particular hair will stand on end—if you have any left. Each cow bellowed for her calf and each calf for its dam—how I'd like to put an "n" to that last word, with cow to top off with—and each particular cowboy yelled as though he were six, and interested in his mission. They were trying to ford the stream, not a hundred yards from my head. Of course I was broad awake, expecting every instant that the boy would start up with the impression that a million Utes had come down for him. I opened the tent fly, and the moonlight streamed brightly in upon his sunburned face; he heaved a long sigh of utter satisfaction, turned over and snored an accompaniment to the pandemonium in the road. I gave it up, and prepared to turn in again just as the rear end of the cavalcade was passing out of sight.

But not to sleep, just yet. My friend has a dozen or more burros, and the burro is another of the blessings of this world for which I possess unlimited love. Their patient and melancholy looking eyes will excite the sympathy of any human save the miner; their ears are a mystery; their song! — Oh for a bard to string his lyre and sing in poetic numbers his praises of the burro's song! I have sometimes thought the burro the Pegasus of some of our Colorado poets, but that they shunned their source of inspiration; gave him the cold shoulder, as it were. Rivalry begets jealousy, and that may account for it; each individual poet would swear by himself only, upon the same principle that every fellow likes to take to himself the credit of all the good things said and done, forgetting there is nothing new under the sun.

Well, my friend's burros had ranged themselves in line along the inside of the lane fence, and with their ears sticking straight out a foot or more between the top rails, seemed to be silently investigating the cause of the misery in their vicinity. A little blue fellow at the head seemed to take in the situation, as the last cowboy galloped by; then he stuck his head through the fence rails and laughed; his immediate neighbors of course saw the joke, and joined in. The whole band at once became inspired, and that infected me. When it grew monotonous, I began "heaving rocks;" they pulled their heads in at this unexpected interruption, backed off a few rods out of the reach of my compliments, and stared at me with their ears. After apparently taking in *my* situation, they began laughing again. I laid down in disgust, and the boy slept on. The moon was going down in the West before the serenade entirely ceased; then I went to sleep, and dreamed—no wonder, you say—that I was in Ireland. There I met the Doctor, driving round in an American buckboard, with no tires on the wheels. I asked him where the irons were, and he told me the English Government was covering the Green Isle with railroads as a military necessity, and was confiscating all the iron. Building railroads being then my mission, I had a gang of men at work, when I felt myself suddenly hit in the back with a spike hammer, whereat I was broad awake in the tent on the bank of the river, and the boy's knees planted in my ribs. I shook him, gently of course, and asked him why he did it. He said he didn't know, but guessed he was asleep; that he could always do it at home, and strike his knees against the wall. There was no answer to this, so I told him to go to sleep again, which he did. In less than five minutes he was lying crosswise. I straightened him out, gently of course, and he wanted to know why I did that. My explanation being satisfactory, he went to sleep again, and I was getting into a doze when he turned a somersault and lit with his head in my stomach. I straightened him out again, gently of course, and asked him if he thought I was a circus ring. He said he had been dreaming. I told him he shouldn't dream; that dreaming was the peculiar privilege of his elders. I might have read him quite an essay on dreaming, but he was having out his morning nap, and I turned out quite refreshed. When I went to call him to breakfast, he was on his knees with his face buried in his hands, and his hands on his pillow. Of course I hesitated to disturb him in that Oriental attitude of devotion, but I soon discovered he was asleep, finishing that morning nap. As soon as he was fairly awake he began to whistle.

The boy, the pony and I went back to the stableman today, and the latter offered me thirty dollars for the pony, saddle and bridle. I told him I thought thirty dollars rather an extravagant expenditure for a week's use of a pony, but the man seemed to have forgotten that he had sold him to me. When I reminded him of the fact, he said he couldn't buy and sell horses without making something; that the buying and selling of horses was his business; that he had a family to support and expenses to meet; but seeing as how I was anxious to sell, though he had no particular use for a pony, and as long as it was me, he'd give me thirty-two fifty for the outfit. I had finally learned the value of the pony, and being loath to impose upon him something that he did not need, I concluded not to sell, notwithstanding the sidesaddle and the ability of the pony to consume himself monthly. The boy approved the plan—that is all this emergency demands. I shall yet "fish off'n that pony."

The dining room of the caravansary where my boy takes me to get our daily bread is presided over by a goddess possessed of a pink cotton gown and a Grecian nose with a mole—an exquisite sorrel mole with two sable hairs pendant. Looked at from any point of the compass she resembles a shingle with an old-fashioned candle extinguisher for a head. The former physical peculiarity is the result, I presume, of the Mother Hubbard cut of the cotton robe; the latter, of the manner in which she dresses her hair. While she served the fried liver today, a pensive sadness lingering about her blue eyes exaggerated the mole, and it seemed that both the mole and its owner felt they were out of place. As she stood over against me, with the stoneware platter of felicity gracefully poised in her nut-brown hands, hers was that "far-away look" we read about, and I thought,

> The melancholy days have come,
> The saddest of the year.

Might she not be a New England school ma'am away for a vacation? Or perhaps one of our own seminary young ladies escaped for a holiday. I had heard of such vagaries in other hill countries farther east, and knew that fashion followed the star of empire rapidly. I had never met any poets—might she not be one? Her style of *coiffure* and number seven boot were suggestive of something out of the ordinary, to say the least. Presuming upon the faraway look and my paternal appearance, I said:

"My dear, can I have a glass of milk?"

The look was not so far away anymore—only about three feet, or less; and to me the little boy appeared quite as tall as I, as she answered:

"No, sir; we buy our milk."

I wanted to ask her if I might infer that all else in that hostelry was stolen, but daren't. She left me in this collapsed condition, and the boy then wanted to know of me who she was. I ventured to tell him she was the lost Pleiad. Then he wanted to know what a Pleiad was. When I had explained as well as my limited knowledge of mythology would permit, he wanted to know if the Pleiades were in the Milky Way. In my then condition of mind, the inquiry from any other source would have proved the proverbial "last straw." He pouted on my laughing at him, and threatened to tell the young woman that I had said her husband was in hell rolling stones. Only the promised deprivation of the pony, in such event, averted the calamity.

Sometime during that forenoon my boy picked up a friend whom he brought into camp behind him on the pony. This other boy was dressed in the remains of a shirt, with some other man's pants, strapped to his armpits by a relic of suspender and rolled up to his knees. The iris of one eye was black, the other gray; his hair had the withered appearance of having been cured in the sun; his skin russet and of grain leather texture. He might have been half a score or three in years; if he had ever possessed any timidity the sharp edges of it had been rubbed off years ago. Looking down at me with a Selkirkian satisfaction, he inquired hoarsely:

"I say, Mister, be you this kid's dad?"

"His mother says so, and I have no reason to doubt it."

"Is she the boss?"

"She is."

"Thought so; does she chaw gum?"

"No."

"What! Don't chaw gum! What kind of a Christian is she, anyway?"

"A Methodist—an orthodox."

"Well, so's mam, and she chaws gum, you bet—see that"—and he held out a hand that in its normal state would have rivaled Vulcan's for color; but the combination of pitch and dirt exhibited was a marvel of blackness. "That's her'n."

Thinking my turn had come, and taking advantage of the momentary lull, I inquired his name.

"Tom."

"What is your surname?"

"My what?"

"Your other name?"

"Oh! Hain't got none."

"What is your mother's name?"

"Mam, you mean?—Jane."

"Well, what is her other name?"

"Dunno."

"What is your father's name?"

"Dad, you mean?—John."

"Has he no other name?"

"Not that I knows on."

"What does your mam call him?"

"Don't call him at all—she blows the horn."

Upon further questioning I learned that this scion of a nameless house was a nephew of the young woman who owned the mole. Also that he had been informed that I was "one of them newspaper fellers." I hastened to convince him that however much I felt honored I could not lay claim to the distinction. At this he wanted to know what I was "givin'" him. I disavowed any intention of giving him anything, unless, indeed, it might be a taste of the quirt my boy used to tickle the pony's ribs. Not having an appetite for that kind of pabulum, he suddenly slipped off his perch and disappeared; as he did so the sulphurous fumes from the Springs were heavier than I had ever known them. My boy then had an interview with me, amicable, of course, during which we discussed at length the evil influence of miscellaneous associations, the Sunday school mission and kindred subjects. Half an hour afterwards I saw them together again killing water snakes. I went immediately and turned the pony into the pasture, thinking he would need at least three days' rest; it proved a specific.

That day at dinner I found a glass of milk

awaiting me, as well as the young woman, with a smile, instead of the excrescence, being the absorbing feature. Being neither Mexican nor French, the revolution was a surprise; I carried that round with me all the afternoon without knowing what to do with it. Had my boy's mother been accessible she could have cleared up the surprise in five minutes.

In the evening I sat on the tavern porch, enjoying my brierroot, when I became conscious of the presence of the cotton gown and its owner. She wanted to know of me if I were "stargazing." I began to think she had taken me for a widower and eligible, so I hastened to tell her that since my fourth marriage I had outgrown the sentiment involved in her inquiry. She nevertheless assured me that she "doted on the study of the heavenly orbs," and a minute afterwards I learned—"Oh, my prophetic soul"—that poetry was her mission. She said she had been trying to find out the difference between a spondee and a trochee; I told her I knew nothing about the former, being a temperance man; as to the latter, I recommended Brown's, and offered her one, as she seemed to need it at the moment. But she declined, as I thought, in a manner unnecessarily formal. Then she informed me that she had no reference to bronchial difficulties or their remedies, but to feet. I expected no less than a dissertation on corns, that being a tender subject with me, and hastened to express my interest. I became convinced in a moment that I had verily "put my foot in it" for the second time, when she told me she meant "poetic feet." I was about to say something, but felt out of my depth, and refrained, lest I might disappear, head and ears. She then informed me that a spondee was a foot, but whether it was a foot of two short syllables and a long one, or two long ones and a short one, was what "bothered" her. I told her the subject was too long for me to get round, and, in short, that I had never read any poetry but that of Walt Whitman. She had never heard of him, and wanted a taste of his quality; I gave it her:

> My head slews round on my neck;
> Music rolls, but not from the organ;
> Folks are around me, but they are no
> household of mine—

She interrupted me at this point, and wanted to know what I was "giving" her, and whether I called that poetry. It became my duty, of course, to assure her of my utter inability to express an opinion. Thereupon, in a burst of confidence, she informed me that, as I had no appreciation of poetic numbers (though she possessed "piles of manuscript"), she had just finished "An Essay on Time." The subject being prose, and original, I begged the favor of hearing it. She began without hesitation:

"Once more has the earth completed its circuit round the burning and brilliant luminary of heaven; the wheels of Time still roll on and bury every moment in the dust the wrecks of former revolutions—"

Just then my boy came with the announcement that he was sleepy and wanted to go to bed. It is difficult to resist a boy's appeal, as a rule; of the sleepy boy an impossibility. If not yielded to at once, he repeats his invocation every half minute until success crowns his efforts. But I could not go without exacting a promise that, at some future time, when she had time, the Essay on Time, "whereof by parcels I had something heard, but not intentively," she would "dilate" fully. Of course she promised, but the Arctic smile which beamed upon the boy would have made his mother wretched. The next morning at breakfast he complained to me that his coffee tasted salty. I had learned of him that he had already that morning corroborated to the aunt my denial to the nephew of the editorial dignity charged upon me by that youth the day before. I had no milk for dinner that day, nor any day thereafter; the faraway look came back into Merope's eyes, and, for me, was stereotyped there. The Essay on Time was lost; so were I and the boy—at least we seemed to be the only ones aware of our own presence at meal times. I always have sympathy for those who realize having, as it were, "wasted their sweetness on the desert air." But the young woman ignored sympathy, and I was made painfully conscious of my inability to eat her pearls. One's pride may sometimes exert the mastery over one's appetite, but a boy's stomach, especially a healthy boy's, possesses no such armor. His tyrant began to dictate to him, and, as tyranny generally begets rebellion in the subject, there was no alternative but to declare war or vacate. Being always peacefully inclined, I adopted the latter, and the boy, the pony and I took our leave.

He's No Sardine

Wagon Wheel Gap ought to have been colonized by Frenchmen. Why, did you say? Well, the Gap proper is a few hundred feet long. On the southwest side of the Rio Grande, a cliff, about six hundred feet at the base, reaches heavenward perpendicularly about the same distance. Opposite, and stretching for two miles or more down the stream, is a beetling wall, in some places, they tell me, thirteen hundred feet high. To reach the summit, one must go two miles up the river to Bellows Creek, strike into a game trail that leads through numberless little parks, bordered with mountain pines, and gorgeous with the hues of wildflowers. If a Frenchman should walk to the summit of his ambition, he would be too tired to fall off; if he rode up, being a mercurial creature, he'd have time to, and would, change his mind, go back to his family, if he had any, and wonder why he had ever entertained the notion that this is not a good world to live in. Looked at from below, there would be such a fascination in the absolute magnificence of the means to his end, that when the melancholy fit enraptured him again, he'd go over the same trail, with the same happy result. With those cliffs hanging over him, the consequences of charcoal, morphine, the pistol or the rapier would become coarse. He would abandon all other routes to immortality, and finally die in his bed with the weight of years, like a Christian. That was my explanation to the Captain, and he believed in it, as we lay peering over the edge and looking down at our six-feet friends turned into midgets.

Those friends of ours, good rodsters all, stood on the bank of the river, evidently predicting what a day might bring forth. The Rio Grande was metamorphosed from a crystal stream into a river of mud. From our dizzy height, it looked like a demoralized rope, the impeding boulders in the current making the frayed patches. We had seen it in that plight and none other for two weeks. But that we had been assured each day that there would certainly be a change on the morrow, we would have sworn its normal condition was "riley."

Having been lied to daily for the last fourteen days, our hope had ended in the faith that inspired our comforters. "So much a long communion tends to make us what we are:—even I" promised each newcomer, anxious to test his skill, that the river would "clear up tomorrow." We had heard, too, about four times a day, of the eight-pound trout captured somewhere in Antelope Park, on a seven-ounce rod—the trout I mean, not the park. I knew all the history of that trout; it had been skinned and the skin stuffed; I saw a woman who saw the trout, and I, of course, had no hesitation in confidently asserting its weight and the details of its capture.

Our hourly routine had been to go to the river, examine the color of the water, and the mark that registered its stage; every fellow said it would "clear up tomorrow"; then we went back to the house and smoked.

Being on higher ground, the Captain thought he would vary the subject, so he said:

"I'd like to catch a pound and a half trout."

I told him he should have one; that one of eight pounds had been caught somewhere in Antelope Park, and that it had been skinned and the skin stuffed; then he said he felt encouraged. That night the river did clear a little, and notwithstanding we knew that every fish in the river was gorged, we could not resist going downstream. Having floundered round on the slippery boulders for a couple of hours without sitting down, we reached a couple of good-sized pools at the head of a riffle; the Captain took the upper, I the lower. Making my way out near to midstream, I took up my station behind a large flat rock that stood about a foot out of water, and busied myself sending a "coachman" and a "professor" out into my domain with a little hope that I might induce something out of the inviting pool. Before I had been there five minutes a yell from the Captain caused me to look his way. His Bethabara was beautifully arched, and at the end of fifty feet of line something was helping itself to silk.

"I've got him—he's a whopper."

"That's the pound and a half I promised you," I answered, as a beautiful fellow shot across the stream not three yards above me; "but you'll lose him in that current."

"I know it, unless I work him down your way."

"Come on with him—don't mind me." I reeled in, climbed on the rock, and sat down to see the fun. The noble fish made a gallant fight, but the hook was in his upper jaw, and it was only a matter of time when he would turn upon his side. Working him downstream, through my pool and round into the quieter water near shore, was the work of ten minutes at least; the captive, seeming to readily understand that still water was not his best hold, kept making rushes for the swift current; but each time he was brought back, and soon began to weaken under the spring of the lithe toy in the Captain's hand. Fifteen minutes were exhausted when the scale hook was run under his gills, and he registered one pound twelve ounces.

Apologizing for creating a row in my quarters,

the Captain went back to his old place, while I again tried my luck. About five minutes elapsed when I heard another, not to be mistaken yell.

"I've got another—he's bigger than the first."

"Yes, I see you have—I think it's infernally mean."

"I know it is, but I can't help it. I've got to come down there again."

"Well, come on," and I sat down again to watch the issue. The struggle was not so brave, though the fish, when brought to scale, weighed half a pound more than the first. While we were commenting on this streak of luck, we noticed a change in the water, its partially clear hue began to grow milky, and in less time than it takes to tell it, a boulder six inches under the surface was out of sight.

"We might as well go to dinner, no trout will rise in that mud," and I reeled up with the reflection that the next best thing to catching a trout is to see one captured by one who knows how to manipulate a two-pounder on a seven-ounce rod.

That evening the river gave promise, as usual, of "clearing up tomorrow," whereupon six of us made arrangements for a trip upstream half a dozen miles, with a lunch in the wagon. The morrow came and brought with it comparatively clear water. We were off immediately after breakfast; arrived at our lunching place under the shelter of some pines by the river bank, it was at once discovered that the river had gone back on us, so to speak; muddy again. No one swore, we just arranged ourselves along the margin and prayed; all good anglers know how to pray. I am indifferently skillful—at angling I mean—but always endeavor to do the best I can. In the course of an hour the river gave us some encouragement. It grew better as noon approached, and after lunch each man was assigned his quarters and struck out for them.

I went downstream with a six-footer in long waders, who was to cross to the other side at the first riffle, which he did. Our flies overlapped each other in agreeable proximity for two hours or more, with indifferent success to either. The trout were gorged with the food brought down by the repeated rises, and seemed in no hurry to seek the broad road that leads unto death.

Finally we reached a magnificent pool, nearly a mile from our starting point, and my companion had worked his way back to my side of the stream. We started into the edge of the pool together, he above me a couple of rods. The flies went over toward the opposite bank, twenty-five and thirty feet away, time and again, without success. Finally an exclamation from the gentleman above me directed my attention from my own tackle to his.

"Have you got him?" The inquiry was made on the score of good fellowship; the bend of his split bamboo, the tension of his line, and the whir of his reel indicated that my tall friend had reached the first stage.

"I've hooked him, and he's no sardine, I tell you—whoa boy; gently now," as a sudden rush strung off full twenty feet of line. "Whoa boy, be easy, now; gently, now; come here; whoa! confound your picture! whoa boy; gently; so, boy."

Just then a call from behind us announced the arrival of the balance of the party. They had got out of the wagon and were standing along the bank.

"Maybe you think you are driving a mule," came from one of them.

"Oh no! I'm trying to lead one—whoa boy, whoa boy—gently now; none of your capers—whoa! I tell you!" as a renewed and vigorous dash for liberty threatened destruction to the slender tackle. "No you don't, old fellow—so, boy; that's a good fellow," and showing his back near the surface the captive exhibited twenty inches, at a guess, of trout.

"By George, he's a beauty," came from behind us. I had allowed my flies to float downstream and had backed out to give room for fair play. It was a long fight, but his troutship finally showed side up, and was gently drawn ashore, the water turned out of him, and he drew down the scale three pounds, to a notch. As we gathered around to admire his majesty, I said: "The next best thing to catching a trout is to see a three-pounder brought to creel by one who can handle a seven-ounce rod." They all agreed with me, and our tall friend modestly doffed his dead grass canvas.

Under Difficulties

THE clouds would assemble daily about the summits of the Sierra Mimbres, whence come the waters of the Rio Grande. Prayers were unavailing; the morning brought the usual complement of fleecy harbingers, and by noon the hosts were marshaled in mighty platoons of black and gray; the artillery was unlimbered, the sun retreated in dismay, and the spree commenced. For two or three hours there would be a terribly sublime row up in the vicinage of the granite and dwarfed timber, that would reach down to the lower hills, and with its results set roaring the little rivulets and usually dusty arroyos, to swell the already turbid waters of the beautiful river. The daily dull monotony was wearing; I thought, more than once, that "hope deferred maketh the heart sick," and concluded I had struck the inspiration of the proverb.

The Old Man sat on Jordan's rugged banks, waiting for that creek to clear up so that he could indulge himself in his favorite amusement. He'd been there a week, camped out, restricted to potato and flitch diet, and had not wet a line. His fly books were an aggravation, and his split bamboo a source of misery. The evening would give promise of crystal water on the morrow, and each morning brought with it a stream of thick, yellow fluid. A trout would no more rise in it than upon the heaven-kissing hills that gathered the cause of his tribulation about their cloud-compelling peaks. The fir-crowned hills and majestic cliffs had lost their charm, the grasshopper had become a burden, and there was no more music in the roily water than in the mosquito's song. I presume he has forgotten all about it by this time, yet my soul cried out in sympathy.

But I was better off than he. He had no John to console him with stories of leviathans caught by other rodsters "last summer." John would scorn anything less than a three-pound trout to embellish his romances; five, six, and even nine pounds were evolved in his imagination. I took him for a Vermont Yankee, but it transpired that the Ozark Mountains claimed him for their own, without the prospect of any other place setting up a demand for him when he dies—if he ever does. He is tall and thin, has a stoop in his shoulders and slouches in his gait; his garments, such as he has, fit him — not so well as they would the clothes line; he has a Roman nose and gray eyes, he chews the fragrant "nigger head," and his saffron-hued incisors habitually caress his nether lip. His mouth is always open, and his scraggy beard would vie in symmetry with a patch of hazel brush demoralized by a Kansas cyclone. A few days ago I wagered him a quarter that he could not close his lips and keep them so three minutes. I won the bet, but have not yet realized upon it. John is a booley, fortunately for the rest of humanity.

Becoming a little impatient at John and the periodically feculent condition of the river, I suggested to the Captain a run up to Antelope Park, twenty-five miles away, and a few casts for the denizens of certain minor tributaries to the Rio Grande. The suggestion proved agreeable to him.

The next morning after an early breakfast we mounted the buckboard, and in company with the United States mail for somewhere, a nervous driver and a pair of wild mules, we arrived at our destination before noon. Telegraphic facilities being somewhat limited, our coming had not been heralded. Our driver left us with our traps in front of a comfortable-looking house, but it required half an hour to find the landlord. We had lived long enough in the country to recognize in every house a hotel. We would have taken ourselves and belongings into the first convenient room, but that a large black dog kindly took us under his immediate supervision. It began to rain, but the dog gave no intimation whatever of inconvenience on that score; indeed, I think he rather enjoyed it. The Captain, after we had admired the dog for a quarter of an hour, slipped his hand into his hip pocket. I don't know whether to attribute the dog's sudden disappearance to his superior intelligence and knowledge of the ways of the country, or to the coming of the landlord. Her greeting was cordial when she hove in sight:

"Glad to see you gentlemen suppose you've come a-fishin' didn't know as you was comin' or I'd a had dinner instead of bein' out to see to them colts the last two died and I don't propose to have no more of that kind of business not if I know myself you bet these has been tended to right and I know it they was risin' three year and of course gettin' too big to run loose that husband of mine run away with another woman two year ago and he come back in less'n three months for me to take him back again but I told him to pack and he did since then I've ran this ranch alone and propose so to do she was older than him"—

"Can you give us a glass of milk," I broke in, irreverently, on this bit of family history, delivered without a pause, with the end, if it had any, promising to outlive us and run into the next century, "you can get us something to eat later in the day."

"Milk certainly you can have all the milk you want and whatever else there is in the house to eat 'taint much but I'll do the best I can what's your business?"

"Just at present we are in search of clear water and trout."

"Plenty of trout in the creek though the river's riley and trout won't rise in riley water I suppose you know there's some big ones in the creek one took off a leader and fly for me yesterday but I'm goin' to snatch him out of that hole yet but what I want to know is what do you do for a livin' people have to rustle in this country or tramp."

Having deposited our traps in the front room, I told her I was a preacher and the Captain a Sunday school superintendent.

"Well stranger I havn't got but mighty little use for gospel sharps they don't give anybody's house a good reputation leastways I've so hearn tell but perhaps if you doesn't go psalm singin' and prayin' round here nobody 'ill know any better you doesn't look much like preachers anyway."

The conclusion was fired at us over her shoulder as she disappeared after the milk. I looked at the Captain seriously and asked him if he thought he could stand it for a day or so; he said he thought he could by going out early and coming in late and going to sleep the balance of the time.

The milk was rich and sweet, but a word of commendation inadvertently uttered by the Captain resulted in a history from birth to maternity, and the details of travail of each of thirteen cows, with the condition of their offspring, their present and prospective value and probable increase.

Leaving him to be further enlightened by this disquisition on bovine tocology, I escaped, and with rod and creel started up the creek. Five minutes after, and before I had lost sight of the house, a hail from the Captain brought me to a halt.

"What puzzles me," said the Captain wearily, "is to learn how that landlord's husband had strength enough left to run away; he had three years of it; his vitality must have been something remarkable."

"His coming back is harder to comprehend."

"I think not; that gives me the only solution to the mystery. You see, he must have been a lunatic; that will account for his strength physically, and for his returning. But do you see that pool? That's the home of the trout that took the landlord's leader. I'm going for him."

"All right; I'll wait and see you do it."

The Captain slipped down the bank, seeking the shelter of a clump of willows, and made a cast into the center of a pool, the bare appearance of which suggested the certain lurking place of trout. He did not have out over twenty feet of line, and the coachman lit cleverly, but without effect. Another cast, a little farther toward the lower end, and yet no rise. A third—there is luck in odd numbers—where the water began to break at the head of the ripple, and the landlord's trout got himself into trouble. There was no stiff cane pole with a tyro at the end of it this time, but a lithe Bethabara of seven ounces, in the hands of one who knew the use of it. It was a very pretty ten minutes' fight, when the despoiler of the landlord's tackle turned up his side and was towed ashore; the fish had a remnant of the broken leader still in its jaw. He weighed a little less than a pound, though we had been informed, as usual, that his weight was four pounds, at least.

We trudged up on the creek, crossing four or five times to shorten the walk, until we reached a point two miles from the ranch. Each taking his side, we began moving downstream, snaking out the little fellows, from seven to ten inches in length, until we had more than enough for a late dinner. Concluding that the trout in these grounds might grow a little if let alone, we walked back. The manner in which the catch was served up with warm biscuit, fresh butter, and coffee with cream in it, made the conversation of the landlord interesting.

We were advised, that, had we gone a mile farther, larger trout would have rewarded us. It being affirmed beyond contradiction that the larger fish were holding a sort of salmon tea higher upstream, and the Rio Grande still being muddy, the next morning found us nearly a couple of miles farther toward the headwaters. But if there were any trout exceeding a half pound in any of the pools industriously tickled by us, they must have known who we were, and, therefore, declined an interview.

This kind of sport had not been bargained for; a strict adherence to the trail, with diligence, would enable us to reach the ranch in time for a lunch and the buckboard "going down." We made it, besides having time to bid our landlord adieu, the sound of her melodious voice gradually dying out as the wild mules increased the distance between us.

That evening the river gave promise, as usual, of being clear in the morning, always provided, of course, that it had not rained "up above." But the next day we learned that the customary entertainment had taken place among the lofty peaks of the San Juan. When any man again tells you that "it never rains in Colorado," remind him of Ananias' fate.

A day did come, finally, and go, through all the hours of which the sun had an easy time of it in making things warm; in the evening we could fairly see the boulders in the river, and the next day it was clear. But back in the west the clouds had already gathered, and if any trout were to be captured we could not stand upon the order of our going. After breakfast half a dozen of us piled into the wagon, rode five miles down the river and began operations, which we were satisfied must cease by noon. For half an hour or so the trout raised fairly, and then the casts increased from one to a dozen, and this was finally resolved into a devoted whipping of every likely place without avail.

Toward lunchtime I waded ashore, clambered up the bank ten feet above the river, and stood waiting for my comrade of the morning. He was standing in the stiff current, thigh deep, and faithfully sending his flies into a long eddy thirty feet away. I called him, but the response I received was that the place had never failed him, and he wanted to go the length of it. So I stood watching the play of his split bamboo and the curl of the light silk line; now and then the heel of his leader would strike, but generally the coachman on the end was first to touch the water. He had told me only the day before, though he acknowledged it was beyond his skill, that in casting, one should never use more than the forearm; that to confine the movement to the wrist was still better. The awkwardness of the full-stretched arm swinging back and forth was apparent, but to one unaccustomed to light tackle the habit is hard to overcome. I told him to keep his arm down, and he did for two or three casts; then up it went again, he forgetting the admonition in his desire to reach a few feet further. When I reminded him of it he looked round, laughingly, and said he couldn't. Just then my attention was called to a pilgrim with weak eyes peering out from under the broken-down brim of an old felt hat, sallow as the mug it covered; his butternut jeans tucked in his boots, and his woolen shirt suggestive of other occupants than himself.

"What does a pole like that cost, Mister?" motioning with his head to the bamboo I held in my hand. Being disposed to treat everybody with civility, I told him.

"I don't think anybody kin ketch fish with that 'ar thing, 'cept little ones. I like one o' them long stiff fellers to jerk 'em with; I shouldn't think this here thing was no account," and he gesticulated with his head again. "Now, the best way to git fish is with a net; now, I wish I had a net; look at that 'ar man thar, he'll not git fish in a week."

"Mark you, my friend!" The libel stepped back a couple of paces; I don't know why. "If you catch fish in that way, they will cost you ten dollars each," I continued mildly. "Try it, I wish you would; there is a standing reward of five hundred dollars for such fishermen as you claim to be; perhaps I might get the money and you a rope."

"See here, Mister, I ain't got no net; I ain't goin' to ketch no fish; I'm goin' to Silverton; I don't keer 'bout fishin' no way; hits mighty po' business."

"The sooner you get to Silverton the better — every man, woman and child in this park wants to earn that five hundred dollars."

What further I might have said I don't know, but just then my friend with the split bamboo hailed me; he had made a strike, to his own surprise as well as mine, for the water had become quite cloudy. With his face downstream and rod well up, he was talking to his victim much as one would address a fractious colt. It was pleasant to listen to his expressions of assurance that no harm should come to his troutship if he would only behave himself, followed by a threatening admonition at every rush for liberty. If my tall friend was not skillful enough to carry away the first prize at a casting tournament, he knew at least how to handle and save the victim he had struck. Having quite exhausted him, he was reeled in till the line could be grasped, and the trout was drawn cautiously within reach; the line was then changed to the rod hand, and with a quick movement, evidently not acquired without practice, that trout was scooped up against the angler's stomach; the next movement was to run his dexter finger into the trout's mouth, press his thumb upon its neck and break it, the fish being held in the left hand, and the three fingers of the right holding the rod. Having thus killed him, the hook was removed, and he was held up triumphantly to be admired. The rest of the party had arrived in time to see the close of the struggle with a handsome two pounds and three ounces of salmon-colored luxury.

The misery under the felt hat had departed.

His Sermon

JOHN DOE—and by Doe I do not mean the Doe ex dem. Gorges vs. Webb, nor Doe, lessee of Gibbon, vs. Pott. My John Doe was not a Doe of fiction, but a gentleman of flesh and blood. He was not a great man, it is true, except in the matter of temperance and cleanliness. As he has not gone into history because of either of those virtues, and has no doubt been, in the course of nature, long since gathered to his fathers, leaving no issue, I may write of him without fear of giving offense.

The unblemished linen and highly polished shoes of Mr. Doe always challenged my boyish admiration. The enviable condition of his shoes I could account for. He cleaned them with his own hands, I knew, because I had, on more than one occasion, discovered him in the act. Whatever Mr. Doe did, he endeavored, at least, to do well. There were no dull spots on his shoes, but an exquisite evenness of polish pervaded their whole surface from heel to toe and from top to shank. In connection with the linen they indicated to me the possession by their owner of an always desirable credit. I had been taught to believe that no gentleman ever permitted himself to be seen in foxy shoes or soiled linen. It did not follow, of course, that all men in clean shoes and linen were gentlemen, nor did I so understand it, but that the fortunate possessor of these well-conditioned articles of apparel presented, as it were, a *prima facie* case for my consideration. They were component parts, so to speak, in the absence of which, the accomplishment of the structure suggested would be an impossibility. The garments of Mr. Doe were rarely new, as a whole; a new coat, for instance, was not always seen in his company with a new pair of trousers. Whether he labored under the impression that the display of an entire new suit upon his person would mark him as a man of too much magnificence, or whether the condition of his finances deterred him, I am not prepared to say. But whether new, or napless and white at the seams, they were always innocent of dust. His linen, however, was a mystery to me; certainly he did not himself do it up, he kept no servant and it was not sent out. It may be surmised that I had rather an intimate acquaintance with the domestic establishment of Mr. Doe. I did, and it was not savory—I mean when considered from the broom and soap and water standpoint.

The house of Mr. Doe was the home of odors, wherein the fragrance of boiled cabbage and onions seemed to wage perpetual warfare for supremacy. The pattern of the carpet in the best room has escaped my memory, but a spot in it will always linger with me as fixed as in the carpet. This spot was about the size of an ordinary chair seat, and was always associated in my mind with a ham, a twenty pound ham; as if the hind-quarter of a magnificent porker had suddenly melted its shape into the brown and orange tints of the best carpet and refused, with porcine obstinacy, to come out. The furniture, as long as I saw it, was in a chronic state of immature cleanliness, and impressed me with the idea that someone had been round with a wet cloth, and, having been suddenly called to the front door, had neglected to come back.

Mrs. Doe I remember as a tall, thin lady, in a black calico gown with little round gray and brown spots; and I have a recollection of debating in my mind as to the original color of those spots, and of concluding that they had at one time been uniformly white, and that that time must have been long before I had enjoyed the acquaintance of Mrs. Doe. The complexion of Mrs. Doe was dark, her eyes brown, and her hair, which was abundant and black, always looked dusty and as if about to tumble down. I remember seeing the lady once seated in a Windsor chair with her heels resting on the front edge—at least I supposed her heels were there—her chin resting on her knees and her hands clasped round her ankles. She said to me upon that occasion that she was not well, and when I sympathized with her I wondered whether it was cabbage or onions, or both. But as I have to do principally with Mr. Doe, I trust I may not be charged with lack of gallantry, if, without apology, I take leave of his estimable lady.

Mr. Doe worked in blue cotton overalls six days in the week, as a maker of watches, and walked on the seventh, the weather permitting; or he walked on the first and worked on the other six days, as you please. He always walked with a cane; why, was also for some time a mystery, he being an active man with no apparent use for support of that character. As a boy, I had an interest in both his occupation and amusement; an ambition to possess a result of the one and to join him in the other. Too young, and withal beset by the poverty usually attendant upon youth, to have the first, and deterred by maternal influences from indulging in the latter, were among my tribulations of that period. I contemplated the bliss of walking with Mr. Doe with an eagerness hard to overcome; and I have sometimes felt that the fear of mere reproof, unaided by the respect in which I held the tender branches of the beautiful shellbark in our backyard, would not have prevented my running away. One other obstacle conspired with those already suggested, more potent perhaps than either: permission was a condition precedent to the acquiescence of Mr. Doe.

But there came a day when my best friend was away from home, and I felt emboldened to interrupt my other best friend in the act of putting the fork into the breast of a beautifully browned canvasback, with the suggestion, that on the morrow, with his permission, I would be pleased to take a walk with Mr. Doe.

"Take a walk with Mr. Doe!" The wings and legs of the duck were severed upon reaching the exclamation point, and the blade of the carver was finding its way delicately through the plump breast and becoming dim with the roseate tint, that denoted the skill of the cook, when he continued:

"Tomorrow is Sunday, and you should go to Sunday school and to church."

My bosom became as bare of hope as the carcass before me was of meat.

"What would your mother say?"

"I dunno."

"Ah, you are not certain, then?"

Thinking, perhaps, that he was pressing me too closely in the wrong direction for his purpose, he gave me some relief by inquiring the direction of Mr. Doe's proposed tour.

"Out in the country."

"Mr. Doe is going hunting, I suppose?"

"Oh, no! he wouldn't hunt Sunday; I don't think he's fond of hunting; and, besides, isn't it wicked to hunt on Sundays, and shoot off your gun and make a noise?"

"Perhaps it is, but—" upon reflection, at this distance of time, I think my interrogator was about putting a leading question, suggesting an analogy beyond my capacity to distinguish, except in the matter of the noise. At all events he hesitated—"but, as I am informed, Mr. Doe generally remains away all day when he takes his walks on Sunday—you will lose your dinner."

"I shall not want any dinner."

"No, of course—not till noon; but take a lunch, and be a good boy."

I do not remember at this late day whether or not, upon the foregoing announcement, I apprehended that Mr. Doe might, through some possible contingency, vary his custom, and go walking Saturday afternoon. I did, however, deem it expedient to leave my dinner unfinished, with a view of communicating with him without delay. Receiving his assurance that he would take me to walk with him on the morrow, I went back to my pastry. The sun came up as usual the next day; there had been no convulsion of nature, in our vicinity at least; the morning was cloudless, without any prospect of untoward circumstance to interfere with our anticipated pleasure.

Mr. Doe announced himself at our front gate immediately after breakfast; he would no doubt have come to the door had I not obviated the necessity for his so doing by neglecting my coffee, and nervously anticipating him on the porch. He had his cane with him, and his shoes and linen presented their ordinary, unobjectionable appearance, as if defiant of criticism.

Our course was through the city, westerly some three miles, and out to a road beyond what in those days was called "The Heights." The neighborhood was new to me, and Mr. Doe took pleasure, seemingly, in pointing out various objects of interest, not forgetting walnut and hickory trees, and even persimmons, that gave promise of good things after frost. Among other things, I remember he called my attention to a blue and misty looking object a great distance off, which looked in shape like the Pyramids of Egypt, as shown in my geography. This, he told me, was the Sugar Loaf; and when I asked him why it was so named, he thought because it did not resemble a sugarloaf. But it was my first mountain, and I have always carried with me a pleasant remembrance of it. Our road lay by an old frame house, with a porch and well, at which we stopped to drink. The house, he told me, was known as the "Bull's Head"; why it was so named he was unable to inform me. Finally we reached the vicinity of a covered bridge, spanning a fine stream. He said it was the "Chain Bridge," but not seeing any chains, I felt compelled to inquire why everything away from home seemed to bear titles that were evidently not appropriate. Not being able to impart to me any satisfactory information upon that head, he called my attention to the Little Falls; I learned these were called Little, because there were Big Falls further upstream.

Mr. Doe informed me that this was a good place to fish. Unskilled in the gentle art, but curious, I suggested that it would afford me infinite delight to see him fish. He then wanted to know if I would not like to try my hand; being informed of my inability to do so through lack of knowledge and tackle, he forthwith cut a small pole, and from the hidden recess of his coat produced a line with a float and hook. Having rigged me out, he proceeded to unscrew the ferrule of his cane, and lo! the inseparable walking stick was transformed into a rod; his own manufacture, he said, as he held it out with the air of a critic and pardonable self-complacency. The recesses of his coat were again resorted to, resulting in a tin mustard box well filled with angle worms. Baiting my hook, he stationed me on a large rock and directed me to drop the lure into the gentle eddy beneath. That float, I remember, was painted red on the top, and looked to me like a highly colored bird's egg drifting out of its element. Being informed that to watch it was my business, I did so with assiduity. Presently it bobbed up and down, then fell over on its side, then again bobbed up and down as though it were sentient and in sound of a fiddle exuding a hornpipe. I inquired of Mr. Doe the meaning of this, and was admonished by him to "look out," that I had a nibble. Of all things desirable to me at that crisis, next to a bite, was a nibble. There was contained in it a fund of encouragement absolutely infinite, that left hope in the distance and resolved itself at once into faith.

"Now, jerk!" exclaimed Mr. Doe, as the float started off rapidly and suddenly disappeared. I jerked. And behold! a bit of burnished silver but little longer than my hand, its dorsal as suddenly expanded as if moved by electricity, standing stiff and defiant upon the sudden change of elements, only a shade duller than the sun's rays, as it flashed into the light—my first white perch, and my initial piscatorial triumph. Proud! The result of the accomplished details of section two of article two of our glorious bulwark announced to the fortunate choice of the majority of the unsoaped out of the seventeen millions and odd of the free and enlightened, placed him upon no loftier ground; I would have patronized His Excellency at that sublime moment.

"It was born in you," said Mr. Doe, as he relieved the captive and placed him in my outstretched hands. My perception of Mr. Doe's meaning was intuitive, and I suggested that I would like conviction impressed upon the mind of my other best friend by a personal examination of this peerless perch. Nothing could be more easily accomplished; it was slipped on a stout string and consigned to an isolated pool. During the ensuing hour my attention was divided between the jail of my captive, the red-top cork and the actions of Mr. Doe; that gentleman had stationed himself a few yards below me, and had secured quite a respectable string of perch, while I had added several, beside two tobacco boxes, to my own.

At lunch it dawned upon me to inquire of Mr. Doe if he did not think it wicked to fish on the Sabbath. My recollection is that he felt loath to set himself up as a judge in the matter. But the leaping stream, the picturesque rocks, the trees and sweet air had attractions for him, and he could enjoy them but one day in seven; for those who had nothing else to do the case might be different; he thought that perhaps education had much to do with the matter—"One man esteemeth one day above another; another esteemeth every day alike. Let every man be fully persuaded in his own mind," said Mr. Doe.

Somehow it crept into my youthful imagination, as I listened to him, that the beautiful river, the rocks and the trees, had been created for him, but that he claimed no monopoly. Yet no rich man could purchase them nor deprive him of his property; that for this he was thankful, and entertained for the philanthropic Creator of these the same sort of reverence, but in a new and quiet way, that I had been accustomed to hear must, to be acceptable, be expressed within doors. And I wondered, if he should be so unfortunate as to die then and there, whether he would go to heaven. My doubts as to myself, and the propriety of my participation in his peculiar worship were grave in the extreme.

The doubts, however, did not prevent my renewing the fascinating occupation of the forenoon, and thereby adding a few more victims to my already questionable spoils.

The shadows began to lengthen and grow quite grotesque in their attenuation, before I inquired of

Mr. Doe as to his intentions about returning. He gave as his reason for not going sooner that he deferred to the prejudices of others to the extent of avoiding any aggressive expression of his own opinions, by trailing his fish through town in daylight. That while he saw no impropriety in passing the Sabbath outdoors in the fresh air and sunlight, there were those who would be shocked at what they deemed a desecration. He felt responsible to a higher authority for his acts, and would render his accounts at the proper forum in due course of time. Meanwhile he proposed to follow the admonition of the great apostle: "*If it be possible*, as much as lieth in you, live peaceably with all men." Upon this he transformed his rod again into a walking stick, carefully stowed away the lines, and threw the remaining bait into the stream; we gathered up what had been vouchsafed us and started for home.

The condition of Mr. Doe's mind was unquestionably tranquil, while mine was encumbered with doubts, yet devoid of apprehension, in the matter of serious consequences, at least. Our walk home was accomplished satisfactorily, the latter part of it being in the dark through the neighborhoods where we were best known, the twilight being short in that latitude and gas then only a possibility. He who had given me permission to go walking expressed severe astonishment at the evidences of the day's doings presented to him. Mr. Doe was not a large man, but his shoulders were broad; he improved upon our original ancestor by assuming the responsibility. My enthusiastic portrayal of the delights experienced were listened to, I thought, with interest; I did not go supperless to bed, and I had some of the fish for breakfast. The diet was no novelty, but the flavor upon that occasion far surpassed that of any former experience, and no fish since has tasted so sweet as that first perch. The burnished silver tint had given way to an exquisite brown, delicate as the hue of an amber cloud painted by the evening rays of an autumn sun. Crisp, and with a fragrance to subdue the censorious palate of an epicure, he invited me to remove his dorsal, and lay bare in equal halves the firm, white meat; next, without a hair'sbreadth torn, the backbone cleaved as smoothly as a type from its matrix, and appetite and palate joined in adulation. I would cherish the memory tenderly, but, above all, the text and sermon of Mr. Doe.

BOURGEOIS